A Roof of Red Tiles
& other stories & poems

Rowan B Fortune
(editor)

INDEPENDENT INNOVATIVE INTERNATIONAL

Published by Cinnamon Press
Meirion House
Glan yr afon
Tanygrisiau
Blaenau Ffestiniog
Gwynedd LL41 3SU
www.cinnamonpress.com

ISBN 978-1-907090-40-0
British Library Cataloguing in Publication Data. A CIP record for this book can be obtained from the British Library

Designed and typeset in Palatino and Garamond by Cinnamon Press.
Cover design by Jan Fortune-Wood from detail of original artwork 'Man and Woman' © Dileep Kumarvs agency dreamtime.

Cinnamon Press is represented by Inpress and by the Welsh Books Council in Wales.

Printed in Poland

Introduction

Fractured narratives and linguistic play, revelations and imploding realities; short stories and small poems are potent mediums, especially for a society in which so much is postponed by work, mindless leisure and ready-made culture. They can pierce life—force us to see as much as live, to take delight or discomfort (or delightful discomfort) in reflecting on the human condition. To reference the philosopher Raymond Tallis, these stories break the chain of *and then, and then, and then*; there is a *now* and a *here*.

A Roof of Red Tiles unites a diversity of prose aesthetics. Joanna Campbell's 'Bonanza Tully's Baby' subverts expectation with a wry humour; an idiosyncratic Southern Gothic told in first person vernacular. Catherine Coldstream's 'No Sugar' depicts desire sublimated as religion with a caustic psychological realism. Jane McLaughlin's winning story is of motherhood, freedom and desperation, set in a richly described Tuscany. From the first line it is vivid and vital, 'A woman in winter, pushing a baby down a cold street.' The prose is tactile, sensory and there is a focus on unnoticed minutia, 'The child's eyes open, dark and blue-clouded, and she looks up into the woman's face. She moves her mouth as if sucking, her small hands wave rhythmically.'

Louise Warren, the winning poet of the Cinnamon Press Poetry Competition, possesses an incredible precision and originality of language, 'their smiles blown out.' In her sequence 'Nesting Series' she explores eggs as objects and symbols, 'the size of an earthed planet/ And heavy as the deepest sorrow.' They are haunting, subtle, but elegant, 'Each solitude reflects the other,/ showing nothing,/ concealing darkness.'

Rowan B. Fortune
Tŷ Meirion, April 2011

Contents

A Roof of Red Tiles

Louise Warren

Nesting Series

No 1. Egg of extinct elephant bird

The egg is the size of an earthed planet
And heavy as the deepest sorrow.
The colour is beige,
the worst of all sadnesses
and the weight of heartbreak
has stopped it dead,
literally. And no one notices.

No 2. Storm Petrel

Perched in the corner,
down the corridor, past the dinosaurs,
the insects,
the magma of children,
is a box with a bird in it,
dead,
with a fixed terrified eye.
Underneath, in a hollowed out burrow
a hole with an egg in it,
tiny.
Anyone could take it.
Take it.
The bird can do nothing.

The Reverend H.A. Macphearson
billows along the cliff.
A great dark, towering cloud of a man,
swooping down.

The bird, pressed by the wind onto the grass,
squeezed half dead by it.

The cloud man taking out the sun like an egg
and putting it in his black pocket.
The emerald grass
iridescent as a wing, laid out flat
against the rising ruffling grey plumage of the sea.
The bird dies.
The Reverend has it
cups it tenderly in his hand
then hands it to the nation.

Small parcel of bird arrives in London.
Stuffed.
Nesting Series Number 95.
Storm Petrel.

No 3. Three white eggs

Perfect stillness, three white silences
hold my gaze,
fixed with a cold lunar intensity,
we are separated only by glass.

Each solitude reflects the other,
showing nothing,
concealing darkness.

Distant, reclusive, celibate worlds.

Excavations

It came with the house.
A lungful of earth coughed up
with all the disturbance, the laying of foundations,
the sinking of drains,
and so it was pushed to one side and left.

The leaves taste different up here, sour.
I do not come when my Mother calls me.
She wipes the light from the doorway
in her neat Capri pants,
her slip on smile.

I watch her fade between the stalks
as the sky hardens into bone.

I am dragging it up again.
I am pulling it up by the roots of my hair.

A Child's Last Picture Book of the Zoo

That last roar is burning up the trees,
setting the whole page on fire,
yellowing the edges of the sky.

The air stiffens,
it is past my bedtime,
and beyond the railings
empty concrete basins gather up the shadows of
hippos and seals,
an elephant folds into a corner
diminishing slowly under the damp moon.

Where are the tigers?
They will not eat you. Blood rusts over,
thin ribs of light stripe the floor, a bare mouth.
They cannot eat you.

Stick heron, penguin suit flapping on a nail,
no one comes to visit, holding a sugar bun,
the gates are shut, only the wind
sharp and hungry, runs out snapping at my hands,

wild dark prints litter the paths, leap and scatter,
the park is swarming,
stink of mould, of rot,
don't tell me how it ends.

Punkie Night

So the children unpack their ghosts,
lay them out upon beds

of white mist above black fields,
a flat unhurried landscape.

Folded back, a grave,
tucked in, a pulled down sky,

silver cuts of water, beheaded trees,
a raw wind, raw uncooked moon,

the children dangling grins,
their ghosts following like little pale breaths.

Later they will sleep, their smiles blown out.

A Roof of Red Tiles
Jane McLaughlin

A woman in winter, pushing a baby down a cold street. Something misty and insubstantial about her, dressed in a pale grey coat with white hat and a lacy white shawl around her shoulders. She walks slowly, her pale blue eyes fixed somewhere in the air in front.

What she remembers now is that even in May the sun drew out the scents from the flowers and leaves. Lavender, thyme, rosemary, crowded in unruly patches around the garden. Sometimes she closed her eyes and followed the drift of the scent, eddying and pooling in the warm air, leading her from bush to bush.

Melon-coloured walls, old and flaked by the sun, but still vivid in the southern light. A roof of red tiles. White shutters, the paint flaking too, closed against the sun.

The house is small, set on the slope of a hill. Below it is a space of scrub and shrubs, a few big aloes spreading their toothed leaves. Then the groves of olives and the vineyards, the archetypal Tuscan landscape, narrow cypress trees here and there. Lower on the slopes several *fattorie,* their red roofs and outbuildings rising above the groves. Although she is alone in the house with the baby, the landscape speaks everywhere of hands and people: olive groves, orchards, vegetable gardens, vineyards, paddocks. The roofs of farmhouses and the hilltop villages that crown two of the surrounding hills.

A Toyota, an old model with a British plate parked in front of the door. The sound of a small baby crying inside, which stops after a few seconds.

The nights have been brilliant with a full moon growing over the last few days, now a clear whiteness over the landscape.

She sits with the shutters open, long hours into the night, looking at the moonlit landscape, the olive groves pewter grey, the thin sharp cypresses starker black than ever. Nothing human ever moves, just a few horses stirring in a paddock down in the valley, their manes and flanks catching the moonlight.

Beside her a Moses basket in which a baby girl sleeps. When the child wakes she picks her up and puts her to the breast, still looking out over the valley as the baby feeds. She marvels at the strength in the baby's mouth, the way the muscle of it clamps and draws on her nipple, at the single-mindedness of this quest for food, the way the child will root and snuffle if she cannot find her milk at once. Then its one desire fulfilled, it will relax, its obsidian eyes distant and unfocused. She will stand again at the window, the baby's head against her neck like an apple warmed by sun until the breathing grows more shallow and even and she sleeps. Then she lies her gently back in the basket and covers her with a sheet.

Her days are much the same. It is all she has ever wanted.

The garden is full of tomatoes, aubergines, kale planted in the winter, and a few carrots. There is firewood and a few winter vegetables in the cellar and at the back of the house a clear spring splashes into a cistern. She needs almost nothing from outside. But the money is nearly gone.

A woman comes every day. She walks from the nearest *fattoria*, the wife of the owner of the house and land. She brings milk and bread and sometimes eggs and cheese. Her name is Silvana.

Apart from cars on the road and the odd rider, Silvana is the only person she has seen in the three weeks she has been here. But she knows a lot about her family—her husband Fabio, her brothers, her sister who lives in the nearest town with her children.

A morning the same as other mornings. Sun and the smell of herbs. Silvana walking up with the milk and bread. Fabio goes into the village every morning to get them. Sometimes there is fresh goat's milk from their own herd.

She watches Silvana coming up the hill. A woman in her thirties, dark haired, agile, watchful.

Silvana puts the bottle and the loaf on the kitchen table.

'Where is she? Is she asleep?'

The young woman points to the ceiling, to the upper storey.

'She will wake soon. I will go and get her.'

She returns after a few moments with the baby wrapped in the blanket. She gives her to Silvana to hold. The child's eyes open, dark and blue-clouded, and she looks up into the woman's face. She moves her mouth as if sucking, her small hands wave rhythmically. Silvana says nothing, just looks into her face and touches her cheek and small fingers.

After a while the child begins to cluck and draw breath noisily, turning her head from side to side to find food. She begins to make the small fluting wail that is the young baby's signal of hunger.

'I can't give you anything!'

It is hard for her to hear this. She wishes Silvana could have what she so much wants.

Silvana hands her the child. She sits on one of the chairs pushed up to the old wooden table and suckles the baby.

Over the next week Silvana comes more frequently, stays longer. She wants to watch her do everything. She watches her feed, change the nappy, wash the tiny body in a plastic bowl, swaddle it tightly for sleep in its basket. It is unexpected. She had imagined herself alone, all the time, with the child.

One day as she prepares to change the child Silvana says:

'Can I do it?'

She gestures, saying 'yes' and watches as Silvana's unpractised hands touch and clean the child, Her hands are hesitant, but she cleans and calms the baby, singing and talking to it in a crooning voice, seeming to gain confidence as she does so.

The words of a long unheard lullaby sound softly in the room. *Stella stellina, la notte si avvicina…* The afternoon sun has edged past the window frame, casting squares of radiance across the wooden table and chairs, the flagstone floor and outlining shapes of brilliance on the whitewashed wall. The song settles gently in the room, falling like flowers from a tree. The child yawns and falls asleep.

She stands at the window with the child, watching Silvana's white shirt and dark hair grow smaller as she walks away and finally merges into the trees.

That night the baby cries. She cries as she has never cried before, long screaming wails that shake her small stomach, that pour out of her open mouth in unending pain. She quivers as she screams, her small limbs flailing. The woman feeds her, changes her, walks her up and down, swaddles her tightly and puts her in the basket, then takes her out and unwraps her as the crying continues. She does these over and over again. Nothing succeeds in calming the child. She will not look at her mother; her eyes are either tightly closed or looking somewhere beyond her, unseeing as she cries.

Something has broken. Until now she would sit for hours, looking into her daughter's face, the child's unfocussed eyes slowly ranging over hers, to learn every detail, as if it were the most wonderful thing in the universe. And, for the last few days, the muscles in the face learned new ways and something that was almost a smile began to form across the tiny features.

She does not seem to be ill. She does not seem to be hungry, or cold, or wet or in any way suffering. Except that she cries and will not stop. She seems to be disappearing herself into that small black cavern from which the terrible sound goes on and on. She puts the child down in the basket, in despair. She cries herself, to think that she came so far to have this and it is lost.

She carries the basket into the next room where the bed is and lies down. At last, exhausted, they both sleep.

It is far into the morning when she wakes, a clear blue sky outside the window and a chattering of finches in the bushes.

The baby still sleeps, not stirring, her breath coming and going so quietly that it hardly moves the sheet that covers her.

She rises, stiffly, and shuffles into the kitchen. For the first time since she has been here she cries herself, sitting quietly sobbing at the wooden table.

Then she washes and puts on jeans and a T shirt. She goes back to the next room. The baby is awake now, waving her hands slowly at the light, her mouth drawn into a smile. She picks her up and feeds her, but all she felt before seems to have moved into another room. It is not there. The way by which she came to be here alone with a child is a mad detour from the path of her life.

In the early afternoon Silvana arrives. For once she is really glad to see her, to have her sitting at the table with a glass of water. There is something clear about Silvana, her dark hair, dark eyes and rounded figure; a reality and purpose about her presence in the room.

Silvana takes a package wrapped in printed tissue paper from her bag and gives it to her. There is another layer of white tissue inside. Within is something white that she unfolds and shakes out. It is a baby shawl of finest crocheted cotton, an intricate web of patterned stitches, of shapes suggesting feathers, flowers and leaves, of lace borders and shell edges.

'What is it?'

'For the baby. For you.'

It is too beautiful. A gift that has taken months, maybe years, to make, should not be given to a stranger.

Silvana has been married for twelve years.

And she is crying again, for the woman who has made this

18

shawl, and for the child she does not love, and for herself in a strange country, alone.

Silvana takes her hand and strokes it very gently, tenderly.

'Please. I will not take it away.'

When her tears subside and her eyes clear, Silvana has vanished, quietly. The shawl is lying on the table, crumpled like a little glacier, white and unforgiving.

Everything has moved away, except this table. The light from the window and the scents of the garden, the crying of the baby, have become disconnected from her. She does not know how she will get up from the table.

She does not know how the next few days pass. She cannot remember if she has eaten or slept. The things the baby needs— food, sleep, washing—happen somehow. She does not see any more the colour of the walls, the masses of flowers in the garden, the green of the hills and farms.

Silvana comes and goes. Maybe she is doing things for the baby. The baby is wrapped now in the white shawl as she sleeps.

After three days she says, 'I have to leave soon.'

Silvana shakes her head.

'You cannot go.'

'I can. I have to. I have no money left. I have to go home and work.'

Silvana speaks quietly, intensely.

'You must stay. Look, you can stay in this house. We hardly let it these days, people want modern comforts. You can help us with the wine and olives, with the goats. You are clever, you will find things to do'

She can see how much Silvana wants this.

She shakes her head.

'We will help you. We will take care of the baby for you. We will find you a good man to take care of you, someone with a good farm and a nice house. What kind of man was your husband to leave you like this with the baby? Will he take care of you now?'

There are many things Silvana does not understand. Least of all how a woman with a three week old child would drive herself half way across Europe in an old car to stay in an ancient smallholder's cottage.

She does not say, 'He was not my husband. He was not my husband, and I left him.'

19

But she sees a picture. Of herself in jeans and hat, tying up vine shoots on a sunny hillside .Of goats being driven down a rutted road. Of a sunbrown child running and playing between the rows of vines.

She sees another, of Silvana alone in her scrubbed kitchen, shelves full of preserves and bottled fruit and vegetables, pouring her life into growing and making.

These pictures play again through her mind for the next twenty-four hours, turning and returning again and again. Sometimes she cries. Sometimes she feels the sun hates her, and closes the shutters. The baby's features are like a language she has forgotten and may learn again one day.

Silvana comes again, persuading, asking even more urgently than before. She listens, studying the other woman's face, listening to her sadness and loneliness. She knows she must leave before they become too important.

Early the next morning she packs everything in the car and straps the baby into her carrier.

The sun is strong already on the pale orange walls. The scents of lavender and rosemary eddy round her. As she drives down the rutted road the landscape unfolds in front of her with its trees, red roofs, the perfect folds of its low hills, the patterns of groves and vineyards changing as she drives, all softly vivid in the morning sun. She sees the red tiles and shuttered windows of Silvana's house and thinks she may understand what perfect love is.

As she rounds the bend a child, a girl, runs suddenly out of a gate. She hits the brakes so hard the car slews across the road. The baby, thrown forward in its harness starts to cry.

The child is standing at the edge of the road, hands clasped over her mouth, her eyes looking at her, wide with fear.

Megan Wynn-Jones

New Year's Day
for Hal

After the funeral
we go back to your land
near the place of our growing-up.

English winter, and the sky is huge and pale.
Together we thicken your hedge
planting another row of thorns and holly,
your quicker rhythm
taking you ahead.

In the shed you make a fire, we drink tea,
unwrap the sweet chestnuts
you've kept damp in cotton wool
to sprout in the warmth of your kitchen.

In pots of thick dark earth
we bury them
not knowing which, of their own accord,
will burst their skins, pushing up
toward the light

Sue Moules

Women for Life on Earth

1.

Then

At Greenham Common,
I was there because I was a woman,
because I got on the coach
left Wales for Newbury.

I was there in cold winter weather,
scared at the razor wire, waves
of barbs braided over concrete posts.
The strong link fence
tied with ribbons and mementos:
children's shoes and teddy bears.
Beyond that the American soldiers
patrolled the nuclear bunker.

A weekend trying to sleep
in a damp tent.
Our presence the protest.
I got back on the coach,
slept all the way home.

2.

Now

The wood is just a wood,
the wire fence pulled down,
the bunker removed.

Those banshee screams
of unleashed women
and the cold wind
are almost a myth.

Yet he *out, out, out* shouted through the trees
still echoes.

Self Portrait in Shades of Blue

It starts with cobalt from the heart,
a leech of colour to the liver,
turns blood indigo,
moves through the pancreas,
into stomach and kidneys.

There is blueness about the face,
angled from the moon's white
turns into an aura
that spreads over the hands
as they reach out.

The eyes are filled with sea,
blueness that is almost grey
sinks deep down
into the black beyond.

Patricia Wooldridge

Marmalade Forecast

Cooking oranges steams up white
    horses in the kitchen
riding through this fug of daughter,
    to wallow in its
baked dream, bubbling pan and slick
    spoonfuls, orange jars,
where the zest of light clings to the roof
    of my mouth.

Mother and I slip on their waxy moons,
    cellophane hats,
a sky full of milk outside, where her snowdrops
    embroider today's
forecast—light snow and gales at sea—
    losing their identities.

Kate Fox

We Are Not Stones (A glosa)

You're there, I'm here, miles from our happiness
we are not stone, but we are in the grinder,
everything is lost and we are dust and done for.
Barry MacSweeney

He is waiting for me on the beach instead
of the café and carry on carefully aiming pebbles
at a brick sized yellow rock,
like Sisyphus deciding his life wasn't quite hard enough.
I remember the playground girls who were hardwired
to segue into Top of the Pops dance routines on inaudible cues,
whose hopscotch games I might join if I was invited,
and pick out my own rock a safe distance from his,
start throwing pebbles underarm and pretend to be curious
what breeds of bird are flying from the huge rock archway
which stands stranded offshore by retreating cliffs.
He tells me a brass band once played on top of it.
I think we will carry on throwing pebbles while
you're there, I'm here, miles from our happiness, until—

—he lands a direct hit, his sandstone splits,
Game
Over.
He scratches his initial on a jagged, grey stone with a pebble,
etches a star of interlocked triangles on another
and we both look at the stones and
    pause
until he says I should have one too, and lies
the stones with our initials
on either side of the star. As we walk away
he says he hopes they'll reach the sea.
From the carpark I try to pinpoint them,
think of going back later, fear
we are not stone but we are in the grinder

and we are not being washed clean in the brine.
We are not being tumbled together under the waves.
We are not clacking against each other
until one ends up on the sea bed
and one is lifted by cool water to rest on another beach.
We are not being picked up and used as counters
in someone else's game.
We are not being used to build cairns, a dam, a wall,
or staying,
staying where we were left
until everything is lost and we are dust and done for.

The Day That Darwin Died
Amy Kellam

'Have you heard the news? Darwin is dead.' Mary Peck was squatting on the tarmac, rummaging through her stash for the day. The yard was dark and the tarmac filled the hot air with heavy, oily vapours. A rat, grown fat and glossy from the skips, ran noisily along the guttering and slid from view. Mary picked out a slightly squashed packet of Danish pastries and started eating a cinnamon whirl.

Bret tapped his nightstick against his left palm. 'Dead, you say?' His breathing was laboured. On nights such as this it was as if there wasn't enough air in the city. Bret called over his shoulder: 'Did you hear that, Ron? Darwin is dead.'

'For the last time, it's Ronald. You know I hate being called Ron.' Ronald came to a halt, adjusting his belt and smoothing down his uniform. He squinted down at Mary. 'What did you say happened?'

'I didn't say anything,' said Mary, suddenly keen to deny everything. She swallowed another mouthful of the soft, sticky bread. 'Lenny's the one that said it. I just repeated it.'

A man's voice echoed hollowly from the nearest skip, 'Damn it Mary, my torch is playing silly buggers again. I've had enough of this, I tell you, enough! It's about as much use as a lead balloon and it can stay in here.'

'There won't be any getting it back if you do,' shouted back Mary querulously, her face pinched around the thought in a series of creases. 'It's the only one we've got.'

A head appeared over the side, followed by a hand clutching a packet of smoked sausage bites. Lenny hauled himself out of the skip and landed with a thump next to Bret.

Bret looked critically at the packet Lenny was holding. 'You know, you really shouldn't eat that.'

'I know that already, but we all know this stuff is only going to end up in landfill.'

'No. It's not that. It's the smoke flavouring. It's bad for you. Gives you cancer, I read it in the paper last night.'

The vent on the supermarket's back wall muttered cantankerously, issuing little clouds of steam into the yard.

'But what about Darwin?' broke in Ronald.

Lenny squatted next to Mary and put the sausage into the bag she had in front of her. He looked up at Ronald and Bret. 'Well, here's the thing, no one knows. It's official though.'

'It'll be all the pies he ate,' conjectured Bret. 'Bad for the heart.'

'Well, you can ask him about that yourself.'

'You what, Len?'

'I mean you can ask him. He's coming up behind you as we speak.'

The two security guards turned a hundred and eighty degrees to follow Lenny's gaze.

Darwin was walking across the supermarket car park with his whippet Flash. The first thing you noticed about Darwin was that he was short and plump, the second that he wore black plastic framed glasses, and the third that he always wore a hat. Owing to the weather he was currently wearing a white Panama, which glowed gold under the towering night lights of the car park. When he got closer Darwin waved and, changing direction, walked towards the skips. They watched his hat flickering, bright then dull, as he passed across pools of amber light.

Ronald was direct, 'Darwin, Len here says you're dead.'

'Dead? Yes, unfortunately that appears to be the case. They told me last Tuesday.'

Bret gave Ronald a look. 'You feeling alright, Darwin?'

'Well, all things considered, not so bad. Of course, my gout's been playing up a bit but I can't complain, seeing as I'm dead.'

Ronald adjusted his belt and smoothed down his uniform.

'See, what did I say?' said Bret. 'It's all the pies.'

'Shut up, Bret' said Ronald.

Darwin looked about him. He was not a man to pursue conversation hastily. He had always been like that; it wasn't just a trait that had developed with age or loneliness, although perhaps both of these things added a weight to his nature that only a stronger man could have born lightly.

Briefly removing his hat he wiped a plump, pink hand across his brow. 'Good evening Len, Mary.' He acknowledged the squatting couple with a nod, before settling his hat carefully back upon his plump, pink head.

He hadn't known such a summer since Seventy-Six. That year they had moved south: him, Hilda and the baby abandoning the city in a fluster of hope, anticipation and uncertainty. They had been industrious at first: pacing the perimeter of the smallholding, marking plots and fixing wire. The horizon blazed whitely in their eyes. Above, small puffs of cloud shrank, and were swallowed by the blueness. The hawks circled high, then higher and finally disappeared for good, leaving behind a sky so full with emptiness that it made Darwin's head hum. The brown earth paled, grew dusty and stuck to their damp, sweating skin.

Darwin remembered one day when Hilda turned the kitchen tap and the only thing to come out was a bluebottle. When he had uncovered the well to investigate he had found a dark, stinking pool in which two moles floated, thick with mould and decay. The baby had been weaned on that water. He fished the creatures out, imagining how they must have come blindly snuffling along the dried up pipes in search of food. But, all that was far away now, distanced by years, by memory and by the city.

This summer the heat was making the city shimmer. He first noticed this when standing on Hilly Fields, looking out towards Greenwich. Over the weeks the city continued to shimmer with a toxic persistence and people spilled restlessly into the parks, glistening in the heat, their laughter flaring into the dry air like fire and their violence never far behind. The buses were hot and crowded, and no one held eye contact except for mothers with their screaming kids as they willed them to be quiet. Darwin looked out the window, constantly bewildered by the landscape and what people had to do to survive in it.

Last Tuesday, the same day he had found out that he was dead, he had jumped in his seat with a yelp when the conductor asked for his fare.

'Good God, man!' the conductor cried. 'What are you scared of? We are not in the jungle! There aren't tigers here!'

Darwin handed over his travel pass, mute and blinking as the bus went lumbering down the parched street.

Ronald was growing impatient. 'So what's it all about, Darwin? This being dead?'

'Ah,' said Darwin. 'I only wanted a job. I mean I've got my pension coming in, but it doesn't go as far as it used to and truth is, with Hilda not there, I've been at a bit of a loose end.' He broke off to reign in Flash who was nose to floor with eagerness, intent on pursuing the scent trails of rats. Darwin wrinkled his own nose and sniffed. 'A bit ripe, aren't they?' He looked distastefully at the skips.

'You should try getting in them,' said Len. 'It's murder, this weather, sheer murder. Trick is to catch them just after they've been loaded. It's all in the timing, just as with any kind of hunting.'

'I may need to be doing that myself if my pension isn't restored, so thanks for the tip.'

'Just don't ask Bret for help if you climb into one of them things and can't get yourself out again. Ain't that right, Bret?'

Bret narrowed his eyes and carried on tapping his nightstick against his palm. 'Now, Len, it's no fault of mine you went and jumped in that skip without checking, and I'm not having you say that it is.'

'I wasn't saying any such thing,' muttered Len. 'Of course, a man might expect a helping hand if he finds himself trapped without a foothold, but far from me to imply any kind of fault.'

'What you have to understand,' said Bret, 'is that it's beyond my control. I don't have the authorisation to try and get you out of them there skips, so I would be in breach of health and safety if I did and that would cause all manner of trouble.'

'Well, it would have been trouble for me if Darwin hadn't happened along.'

'Happy to help,' said Darwin pleasantly. 'Might never have met you otherwise.'

'Hey, thought occurs,' Len reached out to give Flash a friendly scratch behind the ears, 'that dead people don't usually eat?'

Darwin sighed, running his gaze around the yard. 'Really,' he thought, 'I'd probably be better off dead.'

'It's nice to have a bit of contact isn't it?' he said out loud. 'A bit of a purpose? So, what I did last Tuesday is pop along to the job centre and fill out a form. The lady I spoke to, Marge, was really very helpful. Her lad Robbie went to St Bart's with our Greg, you know?

'Anyway, the thing is, having taken all the information, Marge found that there was a slight hitch. "No can do, Darwin," is what she said. "Bit of a discrepancy. I would love to help you, but the thing is the computer system is telling me that you are dead."

'"Dead!" I said. "You got to be kidding me! I'm sitting here talking to you, aren't I?"'

Darwin glanced sadly around at his audience. 'If only it were that simple,' he sighed wearily. 'It's all automated now you see, for efficiency, so it was entirely beyond her control. That's what she said: "It's beyond my control."'

The group considered this news silently. Bret nodded wisely; the solemn, pendulous swipes of his heavy head pronouncing this to be nothing but the natural order of things. Darwin drew himself upright. 'I understand the need for efficiency. I do,' he said, more insistent now. 'I told Marge that. I said: "If that's what is on the system then that is what is on the system. We both know that I am sitting here talking to you, but what we need is something official."'

'"Exactly,' Marge said.

'"Well,' I said, "the thing is I can't be dead because I'm drawing my pension. There will be a record of that on your system."

'And, do you know what she said?' Darwin glared at them now, with a bewildered disbelief. '"Bloody hell," is what she said. "Bloody hell! Thank you so much for bringing that to my attention. That should never have happened. I'll make sure that the payments are cancelled straight away."'

Some time had passed since Darwin had died: not important or significant time, not history, just a period of disposable time consumed habitually like salt. The days arrived and then departed, like a train he couldn't board, leaving him stood quietly observing as they came and went, his Panama hat always neatly in place. Darwin waited and around him things carried on much as before. The heat demanded space, bullying its way into the city's shadows and swelling in the gaps until the city became lazy and taut. He filled in forms P5 zero zero 67a and P5 zero zero 67b. A week later he also filled in P5 zero zero 3. To think that a form could bring him back from the dead! The idea amused him at first, but as the days passed it slowly dawned on him that his resurrection might not be imminent. His death was causing him a headache: he wanted to go to the doctor about it, but the receptionist couldn't log him onto the surgery system. He found himself growing increasingly frustrated by people's failure to take his death seriously. Would that really be so different if his death were real? The thought snuck up on him sometimes, chased out of the shadows by the heat. When it came he swiped the thought away, busying himself with the daily chores of the living.

'Dead and still doing the bloody dusting! What's the world

coming to, eh, Flash?'

Flash lifted his head quizzically, uncertain of his role in the conversation. This particular day Darwin had more thoughts than usual to send scurrying back to the shadows. He guarded against them with routine; building a fortress from the bricks of habit and cementing them together with a running commentary on the tasks at hand.

'Now, what did I do with the kitchen scissors?'

'I wonder if the washing's dry yet?'

'A nice lamb chop for dinner; that'll do the job nicely, wont it?'

It was the prayer of the lonely, this recital of the everyday, as if the words themselves endowed authenticity, securing with their utterance the right to persist.

'Well, Flash, looks like its time to go and pay Hilda a visit.' Darwin stopped, almost started to say something, and then stopped again. Silently, he picked up Flash's lead.

It was his custom to take flowers. It was expected, but it was more than that; Hilda loved flowers with a passion. She loved everything about them: not just their prettiness but the enormity of their function. She loved how they supported all the crawling and the flying things, the small forgotten workers on whom human life so unexpectedly depends. She loved how each flower contained within it the sunshine that warmed the seed and the cloud that gave the rain. The flower itself was a lovely thing, but its part in the vast chain of causality made it a wondrous thing. If only all things could participate with so little violence and so much grace: that was the ideal Hilda sought in life and Darwin loved her for it.

For the flowers, Darwin picked a handful of penstemons from the garden, which he tied with string.

'Come on, Flash, time to go!'

It was the decision of a moment, mid stride on Morden Hill, to veer right into the supermarket. Yellow roses were why. If it hadn't been for the yellow roses, Darwin never would have gone there. He tied Flash to the railing and went through the doors. The air thrummed with the bright, shiny efforts of fridges, and the sudden chillness made the hairs on his arms stand on end. Darwin took himself and the yellow roses he had selected to the checkout.

'I'm sorry sir, there's a problem with your card.' The girl looked up from her screen.

'I used it in here only yesterday?' Darwin was puzzled. 'It should be fine?'

'I'm sure it's nothing that can't be sorted. Just hang on a minute. Someone'll be along.'

Pursing his lips, Darwin looked about. The queue behind him shuffled.

'Darwin.'

'Bret! How's things going? Must be nice to be off night duty for a change?'

Bret's expression remained impassive as he leaned over the checkout girl's shoulder to read the screen. A second later Bret's eyebrows rose sharply, before returning to their former implacable line of discipline. The checkout girl sat back in her chair, smiling sweetly. Bret's chest heaved and he cleared his throat. He slowly stood upright with a roll of his broad shoulders.

'I'm afraid you're going to have to come to the manager's office with me to sort this out.'

'But why, Bret? Can't you just run the thing again?'

'I'm sorry, it would be easier if you just came with me.'

'But Bret, I haven't the time for this, I'd rather just leave the bloody things if it's that much trouble. I'm on my way to see Hilda.'

'I really must insist that you come with me, *Sir*!'

'I really haven't the time for this, *Bret*!'

Bret took a step forwards, his face as immobile as the white cliffs of Dover. Darwin winced and lifted a hand, momentarily frozen, palm at shoulder like a traffic policeman, his round face pressed into creases: soft, quizzical and dismayed.

And then the world changed. Darwin's feet were pounding down the aisle, his breath short and fast. Damn that trolley! He pushed it aside and sent it careening away out of his path. Damn the supermarket and damn the day he died! He could see the doors ahead, blazing white in the midday sun, opening and shutting silently as people passed. He could see a fat lady, swathed in floral cotton, her open mouth a red halo in her powdered face. His chest hurt. He felt as if he were on fire: as if all the heat in the city was rising in him. His eyes were scalding. He ran, and as he stampeded past the checkouts, his plump arms circling and his hands clutching at the air, it seemed as if there was a burning roar. Beyond, nothing: a haze, a shimmer, and after that the world receded, blank and void.

There was a sensation of crashing. Darwin could almost feel the warm, grimy breath of the city as the sliding doors opened and closed just a fingertip away. Then, as if someone was turning the volume up, sound resumed. Quick footsteps came to a halt at his head.

'On your feet, Darwin. Let's get you into the office.'

Darwin stirred. He lifted his face up from the floor. He was still clutching his bunch of penstemons, stretched out in front of him like an artefact of faith. Gathering his limbs together he rose shakily to his feet. With a firm hand at his elbow, Bret led him quietly away.

'My hat!' exclaimed Darwin weakly: it was nowhere to be seen. The store manager sat behind his desk, clasping his fingers together and circling his thick thumbs.

'Let me get this straight. You tried to use an invalid credit card: a credit card that is in the name of a dead person.' He had phoned the bank personally and there was no mistake: the card had been blacklisted and the bank had issued a fraud alert.

'Yes, but I am that dead person.'

The store manager gripped his fingertips together a little bit harder.

'The card is perfectly valid,' insisted Darwin, 'because it is my card.'

'Even though you are dead?'

'Yes. If I may say so, especially because I am dead.' Darwin flushed indignantly. 'I can't stop eating because someone... some... moron somewhere, pronounces me dead. It's insane, absolutely insane. You must see that?'

The store manager nodded his head. He decided that he saw that very well indeed.

'I've been dead a month already,' Darwin rushed on. 'Do they expect me to starve?'

The manager placed both his hands flat on the desk and looked straight ahead. He blinked slowly, and focused on Darwin. You got the occasional odd one; some of the shoplifters were like that. The manager looked at the card in front of him.

'Mr, err, Anderson, I understand that you were attempting to purchase yellow roses, not food?'

'Yes.'

The manager watched as Darwin gestured with a slightly wilted bunch of purple flowers. 'To go with these. For Hilda, my wife.'

35

A spark of hope flickered across the manager's eyes. 'Your wife? Ah, well, maybe we could ask your wife to come in and help sort out this little, err, misunderstanding?'

'Hilda? Oh. *Oh*. I was going to the graveyard. My wife is dead.'

'Mr Anderson,' the manager gave one last try. 'Is that your name?'

'Yes!'

'Do you understand that there is a fraud alert issued by the provider of the card you used?'

'Yes, because I'm dead! Except that I'm not really dead, as you can see.'

'Do you have any form of I.D?' pleaded the manger.

'Just the card.' Darwin gave a deep sigh and rubbed his temples with a pained expression. 'I think I need a coroner,' he said.

'You mean you feel unwell?' The store manager appeared inexplicably alarmed. The man before him had taken quite a tumble. For a young lad it would be nothing, but there was no denying that this man was on the wrong side of sixty. The word liability flashed through the manager's mind causing him to shudder. Darwin was looking at him strangely.

'If I was feeling unwell, I would be asking for a doctor,' Darwin said crisply.

'Yes, but you are dead.'

'That's why I need a coroner. How can I be dead if I haven't even been examined by a coroner? Tell me that!'

The store manager shook his head and reached for the phone. It was too much for him. It was beyond his control.

Darwin sat in the back of the police car. He had Flash next to him: he was thankful for that at least. They would be approaching the station soon. He assumed he could consider himself resurrected now.

It was evening and the light thickened and cooled like syrup. As the stream of traffic crawled over the crest of the hill, Darwin looked down over a tangle of railway tracks, factory units and advertising hoardings. There, unexpectedly surrounded by flowers, was an old lady hollering. She stood on the wooden steps of a ramshackle house, a veranda of potted geraniums behind her. She hollered and kept on hollering, standing in the lowering sun, shaking an angry fist at the busy road. The cars and buses rolled unconscionably past, belching diesel fumes in a dirty, noisy reply. Still clutching his wilting penstemons Darwin looked out through the window. It was like watching a scene from an old movie that had been spliced to the wrong reel of film: two times, two places, a piece of history that could have gone the other way. As the police car travelled down the hill and under the bridge, Darwin craned his neck to see the old lady flickering from view behind the traffic, swallowed by the city like a puff of cloud swallowed by the blazing sky.

'Have you heard the news?' Bret was tapping his night stick against his left palm.

Mary looked up from a crumpled bag of donuts she had been examining. 'What's that, Bret?'

'Wait, here comes Ron. Ron have you heard the news?'

'For the last bloody time, it's *Ronald*.' said Ronald, coming to a halt next to Bret. He adjusted his belt and smoothed down his uniform.

'What news, Bret?' asked Mary.

'Darwin's been arrested for fraud,' said Bret. 'Well, really, what could you expect, going around pretending to be dead?'

Jacci Bulamn

hands in jacket pockets

An evening beach,
us two in the purple-black dark,
grey sea, nearly invisible stones to walk on
between streams that meander.
I step onto the soft part
as you peer amongst rocks for treasure,
then you stand upright
to look out into the night.
There, a few yards from me,
I watch your thin strip of nearly dark life,
blurred edges, few specific details,
then look around me at the living world,
up into infinite heavens
and back to regard you,
one tiny moving speck of you
in amongst all this.

I couldn't tell if the woman's words were upsetting me

or if I was telling myself to be upset.

It wasn't expected at all.
The woman from Penrith began with a poem by Pam Ayres.
She was good. Even got the accent off to a T.

Then, after one about apple trees in autumn,
she started a piece about drowning.
It was half-way between farce and facts,
quotes from a book back in 1832 about
how to resuscitate the nearly-drowned.

Everybody chuckled.

Lines about scrubbing the body with horse-hair mittens,
putting it in a hot bath,
pumping the lungs with a tube to
bring back breath

and flashing between her words,
calling me like a running dog in the woods, was you.

I didn't know if I should look down,
walk out and light a cigarette,
if I should stand up and protest
or if this was just me being O.T.T.

The audience continued to laugh
and your hands reached out from the river, as if, at last,
you had decided to come back.

Martin Willitts Jr

Missing Person Report in a Newspaper

A man mysteriously disappears from his house,
and doubt lies with the wife. She denies this.
She vehemently declares her innocence
in an age where there is no one innocent anymore.
She could not account for his sudden disappearance
or the absence of his clothes afterwards.
The house on 217 Butternut is empty.
Her explanations were tainted with suspicion.
He left no farewell letters, nor suicide note,
nor degree of certainty, nor forwarding address.
He was a reasonable man of familiar height,
with a fair completion to his words.
He answers to his name.
If anyone knows of his whereabouts,
please contact the authorities.
No reward is being offered.

Some Days

I imagine the world without me.
It troubles me, this knowledge,
and the truth of what it means.

For the certainty of days and the certainty of nights,
there are continuous moments.

Sometimes I imagine you without me
and that too troubles me. So much time lost between us,
so many times when we could have said one last goodbye.

How, too, I think, endlessly, the heart continues
and how it mends itself.

If there is comfort in this, let it remain.
If it troubles you, let it go.
Let the days go like always.

Jane McLaughlin

Darkness

a clearer blaze of stars
never seen, icepoints,
light splintered over a crystal sky

a quiet wounding, slow leaning
into dark water

out in galaxies dark towers
of dust spawn new stars

a dark ship sliding forward
stern rising slowly
from its safe sea-level
until it is a dark tower against
the laser clear stars

and every light
every sconce and candle
every mirror and gilded cherub
every brocade chair
sliding into darkness
so slowly
until flat calm

and there was no suction

stars are being made
out in the far galaxies.

Lights

On the first watch

They noticed whiskers form about the lights
as the temperature dropped.

Splinters, fine frost-drawn needles,
tiara jewels flashing rainbows,
long crystals of ice.
Frozen lashes around an eye.

The firing of rockets, arcing in the starred darkness,
fireworks of despair.

The unfolding of aurora,
luminous curtains across the sky,
shifting and shimmering marvellous colours
over drowned faces.

And lamps, green and red, moving in parallax
confused signals of ships
that could not find a sign
and fell below the horizon
like the westward travelling stars.

Desert Camp
Janet Holst

Alex hadn't wanted to go on the desert trip and had told Martha straight off when she suggested it over breakfast.

'The Littlejohns are going. They've asked us. It could be fun. He's bringing a telescope.'

'May's too late,' he said. 'The camp closes about then. Hot winds.' He was thinking, 'All that way, the heat, one night, and all the way back…'

'Philip thinks it'll be all right, not too hot.'

'There'll be scorpions as well,' he said. 'I don't fancy it.'

She swept away his plate. 'We hardly go anywhere, and it's our last year living in Oman,' she called from the kitchen. He winced.

The camp brochure lay all week on the dining table, beckoning with images of red sand, Bedouins and camels under blue skies, until Alex sighed and surrendered— oh alright then—and now they were 200 kilometres from home on a road squeezed between mountains, the sun baking hot through the windscreen. He glanced at his watch: three o'clock, still driving, and no sign of Littlejohn's Pajero in the rear-view mirror. He felt a venial surge of triumph.

'I can't see them,' he said. 'I suppose they're alright.'

Martha twisted round to look. 'I expect they've stopped at the garage,' she said. 'We're supposed to let down our tires—back *there.*' And she tapped a point on the map.

'I'm not driving on soft tires,' he said. 'It's 50 outside.'

'Philip probably knows what he's doing—he's been here long enough.' She folded the map briskly and sat up, watching for the turnoff.

Alex pulled a face. Littlejohn would have a pump and a pressure gauge, probably a GPS, spare can of petrol and two spare tires. He felt guilty. They'd packed an extra blanket, he'd brought a book or two and he guessed Martha had included drinks; anyway, the camp was barely off the highway, with everything provided. Cars unnerved him. He was OK about Moll Flanders and Keats, and the point of a liberal arts education, but not about 4X4s or tire *psi.* And he didn't much care—let the world's Littlejohns worry. He pressed CD PLAY on the dashboard, and the Spring Sonata swirled cheerily though the cabin, lifting his heart for the first time that day.

Outside, heat shimmered and distorted haze, conjured dragons from loitering wayside goats and mirages that glistened on the black road ahead. It snaked between bare mountains springing straight up from the verge: grey, not the red desert sands they'd come to see. Martha jerked forward, pointing. 'There's the sign! Desert Dream Camp!' And she pressed the console, stifling Beethoven.

He swung off onto a rough track, and immediately they were in sand, grey mountains left behind. A shock, this sudden shift from stony grey to burnt orange that enfolded them in a giant quilt, peaking in ridges rippled and feathered by wind, falling away in hollows, fold after fold as far as the eye could see, and all under an azure sky. He drove at speed, the car swooning, careening in soft glides as deep ruts grabbed and spun the steering wheel.

'You should have let the air out,' Martha said again, and Alex gunned the engine harder. 'It tells you in the Oman book.' She clutched the safety strap, staring ahead, her face unreadable behind dark glasses, as the car slewed and wallowed across the tracks.

'Another sign!' she chirped, and they were veering up an incline, skirting a high dune, until there—up ahead, a scatter black dots—the Bedouin camp. He revved for the final run up. The engine growled, spun the wheels viciously—and stalled. He tried again.

'Something's burning,' Martha said. 'I'll walk up.'

Just as she got out, Littlejohn's car raced past, rollicking to the top. Alex swore, and tried again. More burning—the clutch. He'd walk up, get their stuff later. But Littlejohn, in desert fatigues, cap and boots, was already bouncing down the hill, grinning cheerfully.

'Got sand mats, old fella? Let your tires down?' he trumped through the window. Alex shook his head. Littlejohn pulled a wry face.

'Hang on a jiffy!' He disappeared from sight. Alex clambered out, watched him crouch by each wheel, heard the hiss of air, saw his car sink lower in the sand, felt his heart sink in shame.

'Shall I try?' Without waiting, Littlejohn had climbed in and started the thing. The motor screeched, the wheels churned sand, and suddenly the Subaru was off, bucking and swaying to the top,

45

leaving him to stumble through sand and watch as Martha laughed and hugged the champion.

They'd come without their children, Alex was glad to see. Last time there had been a scene with the Littlejohn girl, who hadn't wanted to come, and the boy kept his nose in his Game Boy thing. Philip Littlejohn was some oil technician: a confident fellow in his late forties, with sandy hair going grey, huge glasses and a pressed, prim mouth saved by determined cheerfulness. Nothing flustered him. He knew about everything and was ready to let you know. Christine was a mystery to Alex: a stringy woman with stridently red hair and a nervous giggle, dressed now in a shrunken skirt and top that made her seem not quite grown up. At least Alex had his books.

'I don't know why you're so stubborn.' Martha said later in their tent, unpacking.

Alex stood fiddling with the key. 'I don't have a pump,' he said.

'Philip probably does.' She was draping things on a wall hook, a shirt, trousers.

'I'm sure he does. And probably a lot more besides.' He tossed the key onto the bedside table and flung open his bag. 'Perhaps you should go back with *him*.'

She zipped up her bag sharply and turned. 'Oh Alex, don't be such a sulk!'

He let it pass. 'Did you bring any drinks—gin, wine?'

'Sorry. Philip will have some, for sure.' She picked up a towel. 'I'm arranging a dune bash. Are you coming?' Her face was tired, sweat-smeared, but he saw she was bent on enjoying herself.

'It's windy,' he said. 'I'll read in the *majlis*.'

'It'll be windy there–and hot. At least the 4X4's got aircon.'

He heard her splashing in the bathroom, the cistern's flush. He wanted no drive over dunes with screaming people, least of all Christine Littlejohn. Getting here was enough: he could now sit and look at the desert, read his book – he'd brought Keats.

She came out, towelling her face. Fresh and lovely, he thought, even without makeup. Certainly didn't look sixty—her face fine-boned, unlined, bright-eyed as she faced him now, arms folded.

'You know,' she was saying coolly, carefully, 'it's such an effort being with you. I'm tired of it. I can't live with you any longer. '

It jumped at him and hit him right in the stomach.

'What?' he said. 'What are you saying? You want a divorce?'

'I didn't say that. I don't know. A separation, maybe.'

46

'For not going on a damned dune ride? You're not blaming me for—'

'No,' she said. 'Not Max.' Her hand reached up to the little shell hanging round her neck. 'It's exhausting—there's no joy left. I'm tired. We've become strangers!' Her voice shook. She picked up camera and sunglasses. 'I don't want to talk about it now— later, when we get home.'

She slipped under the tent flap, and he heard her sandals scrunching on the sand outside. He went through to the bathroom. A single tap, cold, dripped into a stained basin. The shower, cold, poured straight onto the floor. At least it worked, and he took comfort in it.

Over in the *majlis* Martha had organized the dune trip and they were all seated in the camp 4X4—Philip festooned with cameras; Christine, shrunken under a large sun hat; and Younis, the young Bedouin driver. Martha watched as Alex approached, bleached and blinded by the sinking sun, his glasses flashing. Against the desert backdrop he seemed frail, insubstantial. 'We're old,' she thought. Her outburst had shaken her. He was still clinging to the past, had locked himself in, shut down; she, who had almost died of the pain, had dug a cave, slowly healed—she would not let him drag her down. She fingered the little shell around her neck. Max's last gift.

'Are you coming?' she called through the window, but he shook his head and held up his book, pointing at the big tent. She waved, the car revved up and took off, sliding down the steep bank to the gate.

Alex sat alone. He watched the desert swirling, shifting in the wind. 'Where they make a desert they call it peace'—but searing gusts pummelled the tent walls, blasted sand that stung, scratched his face, bit into his ears. Not peaceful here. A few camels lay folded on the sand, backs to the wind. He slid to floor level, seeking shelter and leaned back, pushing away the crowding thoughts. Did she mean it? Would she go? What would he do? He was tired from the drive, tired of talk. His eyelids drooped, his head dropped. It had changed them. Max's dying had built a wall between them. What was there to say, without risking accusations? Your child had chosen death at twenty-three, leaping from a hotel roof in a foreign city. Reasons never learned. Tacitly, they'd sought escape, left a life and its bruising relics, gone first to Hong Kong, then to work in Oman. And the unspoken, the unspeakable, had driven a wedge between them. Did she blame him? No joy, she said. 'Thou canst not ask me to roam with thee where no joy is...'

The Keats volume slipped from his hand. He shut his eyes and dreamed uneasily of desert, undulating dunes and uncertain horizons, camels, and men in dishdashas and turbans—and of someone gliding across sand: Littlejohn, with his telescope; Littlejohn, riding a camel, leg hooked over saddle, rocking smoothly like Lawrence of Arabia to the swelling theme from the movie soundtrack; Littlejohn on an Arabian steed, brandishing silver *khanjar*, and Martha, *his* Martha, veiled, shimmering, tall and lovely, lifting a soft hand; Littlejohn bending, kissing it; and Martha like the moon in wane, fading; the horse neighing, its ears scornful horns... Now Alex himself in rags, locked outside his English home, watching baby Max inside; Max falling; Alex, banging wildly on the glass, begging forgiveness... then waking... lest she should vanish... calling out to the now still, empty desert —Martha! Don't leave me!

'Is this Arabic coffee?' someone was asking at the entrance. 'Do you serve alcohol? I'm dying for a drink.' Christine Littlejohn. So they were back, and Littlejohn's unguent voice, rising smoothly and confidently, 'Tea and coffee will be fine, thanks, perhaps something different later.'

They were bearing down on him, Littlejohn steering his wife firmly: she, frowning, petulant.

'Any dates left?' Littlejohn asked.

Alex gestured to the cushions and asked about the drive.

'Terrifying,' Christine said, rolling her eyes. She collapsed onto a cushion. 'I've cricked my neck. And we couldn't get out, too windy. No photos.'

'Martha enjoyed it,' Philip said. 'Even drove part of the way.'

'That's Martha for you.'

She had come into the tent and was standing by the coffee watching the sunset, her face glowing in the red light. There was something free and unassailable about her, a fierce brightness making him think of a star. She would float away and leave him stuck in his leaden life, discarded, like a rusted anchor.

'I see you're reading Keats.' Philip was flipping through the book's pages as if it were a pack of cards. 'Thought you'd know all this stuff by now. Was he the chap who made a botch of sailing? In Italy?'

'Shelley, I think,' said Alex. 'There was a storm.'

'Always got them muddled. '"Vast and trunkless legs of stone in the desert"?'

'Shelley, again.'

'Not much stone round here, anyway.'

They turned to survey the fading red expanse below. A long bar of shadow crept towards the camp. Three camels stood motionless outside the gate—and behind them an orange ball balanced on distant dunes, streaking the sky purple and yellow. The air was cooler and quite still.

'Look there.' Philip pointed to an eyelash of moon lying low in the sky. 'We should have good viewing… dark enough. The scope's on the dune behind. We'll go up after dinner. You'll need red torches and I've got spares.'

Alex had forgotten. This was why they'd come—the night sky in May.

Alex and Martha had not been to bed. They sat leaning shoulder to shoulder at the edge of the *majlis* watching the morning creep into the desert, the sun's pale fingers inch across the dune tops, pushing back the night shadows to unveil in slow sequence the remnants of last night's drama: the toppled telescope on the skyline, the churned and trampled path to the camp, and the stepladder abandoned drunkenly against Litlejohn's Pajero.

It hadn't been a clear night after all. The wind had brought dust clouds and at dinner they'd listened to Littlejohn lecture on his 24-inch telescope, how he'd got started in astronomy and what they would see in the sky after dinner.

'I want to see Jupiter,' said Martha. 'With all its rings!' Her face was flushed and Alex wondered if she was sober. They were on their second bottle of wine after gin and tonics earlier.

'It's Saturn with rings,' Littlejohn corrected. 'We *might* see them. We should go now; it's clouding, and I'm hoping for some new constellations—'

'He knows the sky like his own backyard.' This was Christine, loud and unsteady, tilting across the table at her husband, spilling her wine. '*Better* than his own backyard, in fact! Do you know something?' She swung around to Alex, her eyes empty and wide, and then back to Martha. The table rocked. 'He's never *in* his back yard! Did you know that?' She flung out an arm, pointing across at Littlejohn. 'He's in Emma Wainwright's back yard. At least when her husband's away—bastard!'

Littlejohn stumbled up against the table, his face white and rubbery, his tight mouth working. 'You're being foolish!' he muttered; then, stoutly to the others, 'She's building a patio.' Christine had collapsed into her chair, her head on her arms in passenger crash position. 'I'm going on up,' Littlejohn said to the silence. 'Is anyone else coming?'

'I am,' Martha said, and she swung herself eagerly out of her chair. Alex, appalled, stood up, dithered a moment, and wandered off on to the sand. He couldn't see any stars; it was all blank up there. You could never fathom the inside of someone's marriage, he was thinking. He would have said Littlejohn had got it right— career, wife, kids: the telescope thing. His own marriage was a tired old habit, a habit of living, not really loving. Or joyful. You trucked along, keeping the rules, holding things together, and then *wham*! It all ended… He heard a noise behind him and turned to see Christine trailing unsteadily after the others. She might have been crying.

He struggled up through the steep sand. He'd probably drunk too much, too, for his sand shoes couldn't handle *this* sand, it seemed, his every step slipping back with a derisive squeak, his calves aching as he floundered on, finally falling on his knees and crawling crabwise to the dune top to collapse exhausted. He lay with his eyes shut; his cheek flattened on the cooling sand, and swore at length. He didn't want to be here, for godsake, would rather be at home with a book—damn the stars, damn Littlejohn, and damn the rest of them! He looked up. Christine Littlejohn lay flat on her back in the sand, waving her thin arms above her head, drawing drunken pictures in the sky and whispering 'twinkle, twinkle little star,' over and over.

On the far side Martha and Littlejohn were joined in silhouette to some sort of giant mechanical praying mantis. He hadn't expected anything so large, a man-size cylinder, with a step ladder fixed to its side. Their voices carried clearly in the still night air, Martha's excited, breathy like a young girl's.

'That's Saturn? Beautiful! It's so big. How far is it?' And Littlejohn's voice, mollified, explained astronomical distance.

'Nine thousand AUs—over 800million miles away.'

'Amazing!' she breathed, as if Littlejohn had invented the system himself, created the whole blasted universe.

'But where are the rings? I can't see.' Her voice carried disappointment: even the planet system, Alex felt, was falling short of expectation.

'They're hard to see right now. It's their angle to earth.'

'Mmm, I *think* I see some, just faintly...I thought they'd be clearer.' They murmured in close harmony: no doubt gazing through the same eye-piece. Martha would love that—seeing eye-to-eye with someone at last.

Littlejohn's indulgent laugh stroked the night air. 'It's a rare sight—they're at their thinnest. Won't be like this again until 2024.'

The fellow knew everything and had likely stumped up here with a ton of telescope on his back, not even breaking sweat. Meanwhile he, Alex, was completely done in. He rolled over and lay with his legs pointing down the slope, his face angled up to the sky, 'the night's starr'd face'. At least Keats had got it right. 'The stars look very cold about the sky'. That said it all, really, Alex felt: the cold, unsympathetic universe; the heaven's dispassionate gaze; the petty blunders and futile agonies of humans here below. 'On the shore of the wide world I stand alone…'

There was a gasp and a sharp scream behind him. A thud and something crashing heavily. Followed by a sob. He swivelled around. The telescope was down. The figures of Martha and Littlejohn on the ground—'the mighty fallen.' He heard Martha scream, 'Philip! Are you—Philip?' Alex rose stiffly. Martha was calling out, 'Someone please help! Philip's fallen. I think he's— Alex, come and help. Something's wrong.'

Littlejohn was lying face down in the sand, hunched, with one arm crumpled beneath him, the other stretched out as if reaching for the fallen telescope or hailing a passing taxi. Martha was on all fours, her face white, flower-like, beseeching.

'He was just talking—? He fell. It all went over. Can you see— Is he alright? God, what do we do—Where's Christine?'

Alex turned him over. It was too dark to see, and he reached for Martha's torch, unscrewing the red glass. Littlejohn's face was spectral, his eyes closed. He seemed not to be breathing, his heart not beating.

And Alex did what he'd only read about briefly, had seen on TV channels that he invariably switched off, his action dredged up from some deep reservoir of unconscious knowledge: he pushed strongly *once, twice,* rhythmically, down on Littlejohn's surprisingly firm chest, that squeaked and grunted with each thrust, *four, five,* Martha meanwhile chafing the man's hand in hers, *ten, eleven,* until the eyelids flickered, and 'Get Help!' Alex had roared; she'd run to the edge of the plateau and he'd heard her calling down to the camp.

They'd carried him down on the stepladder, slipping and sliding in the soft sand and then Alex had gone back for Christine, who lay on the sand, lost and weeping in her own treacherous world.

The morning sun rose higher, colouring the desert. The wind stirred, and Martha and Alex sat on in silence. It had been a long night, and they were waiting for the ambulance that would take Littlejohn back to town.

Martha watched the wind flicking the sand, watched the sand stirring, shifting again, drifting over the night's footfalls, smoothing, erasing, cleansing, till all trace had vanished. The desert opened, unfolded before her, and above it, over to the east, a pale yellow arch lifted the sky with the day's promise. After a while, she slid a hand across to cover Alex's, clutching the Keats he'd nearly sat on in the dark. It was how they had sat in courting days— together, not speaking. He turned to her.

'You'll drive our car back? I'll take theirs.'

She nodded. 'He was lucky. You were—.'

'I was imagining—'

'I know,' she said. 'But it's past; let him go. It wasn't you, wasn't anything we did. Today you saved a life.' She squeezed his hand. 'Hold on to that.'

'We'll go in convoy after the ambulance,' he said. She stood up and kissed his hair lightly.

'On the shores of darkness there is light,' Alex thought a bit later, climbing into Littlejohn's Pajero. Well, he hoped Keats was right. On the road back he played Littlejohn's 'Spaceman' track at full blast.

Sharon Black

Unborn (after Iona)

It's how I always pictured you
—marram-blonde, naked of trees,
your fingers steeped in sand,

lying on a sea-blue blanket, swaddled
in soft grey clouds and sky,
joined to me by bedrock.

You were always going to be the gentle one.
Above the abbey, white pigeons
write your name in cursive script;

waves flutter high upon the beach,
all thoughts of blue suddenly interrupted;
luminous green pebbles shed themselves in the bay.

You came to me too late—me, the mainland,
already with whole civilisations to support,
my head full of earth and clouds.

At the hospital they said your seed
had been bedded down five weeks.
I swallowed pills; you washed away.

Today I leave you again, on the ferryboat to Mull—
in its wake, an umbilical cord of froth
connecting the islands—

and when I turn at Fionnphort you are
small enough to fit in my hand
as if you had simply floated to the surface,

as if you were simply sleeping on the horizon
of someone else's palm.

Equinox

All night she tracks the moon
through the mulch of sky,
watches it wick from feet to pelvis.

She lies as still as silver, offers
the banks of her body
for its consumption.

Beyond the window, night creatures
shuffle in the cut grass.

Soon it will be harvest.
High water. Howling leaves.

Will-o'-the-Wisp

It drifts in late when I'm asleep
disturbs the shadows
traces luminous maps on my back

of the places it has been: in my dreams
it is fathoms deep
its fingers under the covers

are the sway of cord grass
at the fringe of a marsh. Sometimes
I sense it on waking like a brackish stain

in the air; I swallow its incantation
but by dusk it is almost forgotten.
Only when undressing

do I notice the trail of stars down my belly
the constellations on my thighs
the taste of salt on my cracked lips

and I find you kneeling before me, reaching out in the half-light
soaked to your waist
with no idea how you got here.

Josh Ekroy

Plunder

When we neared the barracks we glimpsed
three men with hardened faces who reminded
me of a picture in *The Dying Bush* by Jawad Salim.

They worked in rotation to dig up the ground
by the palace that had been constructed
when Sulaiman Basha was governor of Baghdad.

There were the tiles on which Hassan Basha had walked
as he contemplated his victory over the Sufis
surrounded by his Circassian Mameluks.

We shouted when we saw the looters, and at once
Muhammad Namuq Pasha, Abdel-Baqi al-Amari,
Yassin Hashimi, Sheik Dari and even Sir Percy Cox

all shouted with us: What are you doing, racketeers?
You are destroying the house of your forefathers.
One of the men put down his axe, embarrassed,

pointed to his mouth as a sign of hunger.
As we approached we saw the half-sprung
cables in the ditch that they intended to barter

for scrap. Then we understood everything
could be plundered: the Ottoman cannons by the gate
of the Defence Ministry; the gate's hinges

which every coup-maker had swung open to confute
Iraqi destiny; even the old clock of the barracks
which recorded the times of all their violations;

Sumerian texts from the national library. A tank
stands between two statues in front of the museum.
After what has been lost, what does it protect?

Rosie Shepperd

The girl you saw

wasn't me. That girl you saw crossed over Piccadilly, wearing tan
                                        Roman sandals,
a loose white shirt, drawn tight on a full blue skirt. That girl, who
                                        carried the scent

of gardenias, her lips smiling some colour that isn't deliberate; that
                                        wasn't me. That
girl had amber eyes, that girl whistled top C for a cab and waved to
                                        the man who

delivers on a Yamaha bike. It wasn't me who spread a red spotted
                                        shawl on cool
grass in Green Park, unpacked pippins and bread, spiced meat and
                                        cheap wine.

You notice she waited for no one, threw grapes in the air and sank
                                        her sharp teeth
deep into a picnic for one? That girl, she slept full stretch in the sun,
                                        with a hand in

the pages of Bonjour Tristesse. I wouldn't read that, not outside, not
                                        a slim book that
might make me cry. I've never wiped my face with the back of my
                                        hand, my left hand.

That girl, she laughed at herself, made a Viennese couple jump round
                                        and try to join
in her day. Did you see her stand quite still with her arms held high
                                        for ten or twelve

seconds, then pack up her things with peaceful hands? She looked at
                                        her watch, the
watch I don't wear. So you see, it couldn't have been me who pushed
                                        a curl of thick

hair from her face and strolled with no map towards Devonshire
                                        Gate, licking two
then three fingers and brushing small traces of salt and white flour
                                        from her cheek;

her right cheek. What did I tell you? How many things did I never
                                        tell you? Know this
now; you'll never dream of this girl as me, just as you don't live in
                                        my dreams as you.

A weekend alone in Paris makes no difference at all

The rattling lift at the Hotel St Boniface,
                my too-tight new shoes,
        turn left into Rue de Médicis,
move towards the lake, the children in tartan coats, their battleships.
      Bretagne, Lorraine, Foudre; the undefeated Fantasque.

          It was warmer yesterday at the Tuileries.

            Light chairs rest on the gravel,
          Table tops are marked from glass tulips of eaux de vie:

Kirsch, Poire. Framboise.

          The air moves as a man passes.
  I catch the darkness of his coat, the oyster blue of his scarf.
He doesn't turn, doesn't slow down, doesn't change pace.
        I want to say it doesn't matter. It isn't you.
  It does matter. They are all you.

No Sugar
Catherine Coldstream

Nuns talk of their 'prayer lives' the way others do about their experience of sex, with a mixture of hidden pride and manifest, or assumed embarrassment. But then, Lucy mused, what *is* prayer, at a deep and sustained level, other than a sublimated experience of that (one gathers) ecstatic encounter? A sharing in the universal force of love, a transcendent *eros*, the dynamism of ultimate and reciprocal attraction? Fresh from her weekend at the Abbey, clean with that unified sense of purpose her visits tended to impart, she was mulling over Sr Agatha's comments. 'There's no love like the love of the Lord,' the older woman had assured her, an eye on Lucy as a potential recruit. Yes, she thought, sitting on board the Thirty Bus as it negotiated its uphill swerve into Pentonville Road, she was right; and the touches of grace had been deeper and stronger this time than on her previous visits. A Silent Eucharistic Retreat. And it was above all in the Eucharist, she thought, that intimacy was most fully consummated, allowed its most unfettered scope, the interpenetration of persons, the mingling of bodies. If only I knew how to open myself without reserve... Lucy looked sadly out of the window.

It had been long, too long since she'd known the warmth of human touch or closeness. And now, well into her thirties and still unattached, she sought compensation in the aisles of various churches. She was promiscuous. Most religious people are. And insatiable; daily Communion had become quite a compulsion for her of late. And it was always a rush, fitting it in before the bus to work, or leaving early and speeding through the noisy back streets of Bloomsbury, often clunking noisily in, doing battle with that heavy door, the priest already at the lectern. And then the noise of shuffling and of turning heads, the moderate and momentary shame. Oh that girl, again... someone had once muttered. An elderly porter at the university hospital, a daily communicant, creature of habit, intolerant of youth. And she'd found her way to a bench in a side chapel, sweating slightly while unravelling her scarf, breathing too loudly.

But it was worth it. The warm glow of candles and the companionship of the statues, all half-forgotten heroes, challenging role models of both genders, once flesh and blood, now immortalised as caricatures. Anthony for the restoration of lost property, Christopher for travel insurance, Clare for PR and effective dealings with the media. Lucy fitted in somewhere between Thérèse, for attention to detail and grand aspirations, and Ursula, the social worker par excellence. In a different social sphere and with different mythic heroes she might have taken Dorothea as her patron. But the future remained dim; where would or could she go as a rather dowdy singleton in a world of thrusting youths and bubbly, gushing girls? Of texting teenagers trading in coded messages she could not decipher? And yet she was not past her prime. At thirty-three she could still pass for five years younger, and was occasionally even taken for a student, her shabby and slightly careless attire contributing to this impression. Ah, jumble sales! she thought, as she sank into the quiet of contemplation, they had been the saving of her.

It was at a flower sale that she'd first met David, one of those church fete arrangements when, rained off and pulling jovially together, they'd all crowded into the parish hall. She'd struggled with the trestles, loosening her grip on the leaking and lopsided watering can before it slid, then splashed, onto inhospitable flagstones. And he'd rushed forward, steadying her hold, then mopping and commiserating, muttering something about her not striking her foot against a stone. And then he'd offered tea, a lukewarm cup in a heavy, greying saucer, one now moist and fast disintegrating biscuit at its side. A decidedly *plain* biscuit… de rigueur for girls of Lucy's calibre, he had thought. And No Sugar. For she was not one of those flimsy wenches, easy come, easy go… and all that. He'd known their type (*chocolate* biscuits, assuredly, for them) and, once badly hurt, was newly cautious and reserved. And while not ineligible for female appreciation, now paid more attention to the inner workings of the sacristy and to the serving of Mass than to engaging with the opposite sex. He'd even considered the priesthood. But occasionally one of those good, solid girls came along, a touch of the bluestocking about her, and he wavered.

Lucy caught her own reflection in the darkening window, as approaching Highbury (she still could not afford The Angel and was somewhat regretfully relegated to Stoke Newington… *for now*, she told herself) and seeing the face of what she took to be a child, she then, with a passing twinge of pathos, recognized the serious, over-focussed features of one who spent too much time on her own, the brown eyes bland behind large glasses, the chignon knotted at her neck in resolute independence. It was the lack, or rather *absence* of make-up that pre-eminently qualified her in David's eyes; that and the scrubbed-clean look of quiet, under-exercised features. For there was a softness, a purity almost, in her face; even if she were a little pale and remote in her responses.

Sensory under-stimulation, he'd thought, not without some accuracy, but in her case an outward deprivation wedded to a liveliness and intensity of mind, an inner life he had yet had to reckon with. The day the flower sale had been rained off, and they'd ended up sweeping the sacristy of florid debris together, she had repaid his kindness with an impressive exhibition of minimalism, a modesty and reserve in the few rejoinders she'd made, that encouraged him deeply. A Suitable Woman seemed written all over her, even to the whiteness of her fingertips; the nails brushed clean, the trimmed edges perfectly symmetrical. A woman of few words.

Now she gazed out at the shopkeepers, busy with keys and grilles, closing up for the night, the occasional tramp at the rubbish bins, the drifting crisp wrappers floating idly amongst the autumn leaves, occasionally blown back into the gutter. She'd half read David's mind, that day. She'd noticed him before (who hadn't? the shock of deep red hair, the almost painfully blushing neck) and had passed him by as uninteresting. The bulkily protruding Adam's apple had done it; there was an angularity that warned her off, shielding her from more explicit revulsions with pre-emptive care. Clammy fingers and all that, she knew she could not face. She was an exacting individual and she knew it and blamed herself for missed opportunities only when all danger of involvement was safely past. But in David's case it had all been slightly different; the script had not run according to plan. And she still didn't know whether, retrospectively, she regretted it. Perhaps she was better off like this.

Somewhere on the west side of London, David Rogers leafed idly through the last of the day's paperwork while casting a cautious eye over the darkening Hammersmith horizon. Half an hour to get to Shepherd's Bush and check the answerphone before heading off for the evening lecture, briefcase in hand, the study lights left on behind venetian blinds. In a world of halogen spotlights and dimmer switches he held fast to his angle poise lamp, his slow cooker and his Baby Belling; he'd never fully left bedsit land behind, and had certainly never ventured beyond the inner limits of bachelordom for more than a couple of weeks. Once, when still too young to have known better, before his faculty of discernment had been sharpened to its now acute level of sensibility, he'd fallen in with the wrong type of girl. Lip gloss and nail varnish. Bad memories. And, beyond that, nothing much to speak of... nothing excepting that slight frisson of interest he experienced when, amid the bulging ranks of the tenors at the weekly choir practice, he'd catch sight of the quiet brunette, the one with the glasses. Sometimes her voice would float out, rise above the other altos, rich and deep, or she'd stop the choirmaster and ask the kind of question no-one else thought of... were we observing the repeat marks, and did he want double-dotting? She seemed to know her technical terms. Yes, his sensibilities were simply acute, not dead.

The series had been well-attended this year. Dr Coverdale, dean of studies, had been surprised at the increased demand for water jugs and chairs, and the frequency with which they had to restock the coffee machines, midweek. An awkward time to be fiddling with plastic tumblers, the corridors still busy... and noisier than he would wish. The Influence of Late Neo-Platonism on the Septuagint had never taken off like this in previous years. They'd done well to appoint a woman, one of the controversial new breed of Anglican clerics, and with an edginess and agenda of her own. That kind of thing could be relied upon to generate a good deal more interest than his more staid and conventional conferences. He was seen as token representative of an *Ancien Régime*, obsolete since the decidedly vibrant Angela Fowler had come along, her erudition challenging the very concept of orthodoxy. Biblical studies had never been so exciting, nor so *fertile*, a terrain.

'So, she's sexed up the programme, has she?' the younger of the two men threw out, over ale and crisps. 'Oh, golly yes' the red haired, taller one replied. He was fumbling with the final quarter of a cheese and tomato sandwich, a crescent of elusive cucumber protruding from its crumbling edge. 'Nothing like the last series; you should give it a try again sometime.' But Darren was already pulling on his leather jacket, checking for messages, and making his excuses. 'Sorry, Dave, I don't find religion *does it for me* any more. I've found the real thing.' And as he circled out of sight, the contours of his backside immodestly described by too-tight denim, David found himself wondering what this 'reality' was. He hoped it wasn't what he thought it was. And 'sexed up'? Could religion, and the safely arcane world of biblical studies, ever be spoken of in those carnal terms? Or perhaps he'd meant it ironically.

'Well Lucy, we've given you the pointers that you need; the rest is up to you. Only you can make that discernment.' Lucy resented the suggestion that she was dithering, and decided upon an excuse, a legitimate diversion. That might buy her an extra year... or two. And she'd have the confidence of a relevant qualification. Hebrew or Greek? She already had good Latin, and practised at least a limited form of it regularly at choir. But was not sure that a purely linguistic study would be broad (or stimulating) enough for her at this stage. And then she'd met Angela. A chance encounter one Corpus Christi procession and the extended chat over canapés at the buffet lunch afterwards. The giggling over gin and fizz. They'd been quite engrossed when David interrupted, his corduroyed presence, the loosely knotted tie, somehow vague and impotent beside Angela's geometric crop, her emerald earrings and articulate, slightly obsessive manner. She had seemed an intense, opinionated woman then, in an almost casually worn, apparently incongruous clerical collar, and had been inconsiderate to nearly everybody. But she'd given Lucy a warm handshake and a brochure for the course, and left her to the mercies of David Rogers. He would 'fill her in' on the requirements and details of the course. He'd been coming all term.

Thinking it over on the bus, Lucy was not sure she wanted to be filled in by David. She'd rather get it straight from the horse's mouth; or rather, from Angela's. There'd been quite a connection (chemistry seemed too dangerous a word to use in this context, and, in the biological sense, did not form part of Lucy's rather pedantic vocabulary). She'd just have time to get back to the flat and collect notes and paperwork... and her new Interlinear Greek-English text, of which she was inordinately proud. And then to make it to her first lecture; she could find out for herself by taking part. There was no teacher like *experience*.

She'd been polite enough to David, but no longer felt free to respond to him as she had done two years ago. His intentions then had been too obvious, the Adam's apple too overt, its angular movements when he spoke, the alarming ginger hairs, slightly raised upon his wrists, too visceral, uncontrolled. He wanted her too much, she could see that. And that would never do. After the discomfort of the second date and the embarrassment of casserole at his rooms in Shepherd's Bush, she'd decided to draw a line. He'd offered her his mouth and she, she had tasted, momentarily, the flavour of his longing for her, the odour of his appetites. She did not need to think long about it; the disgust had said it all and warned her off. Tonight she would speak to him and be friendly, but would concentrate on Angela and the course.

'So, where the Greek Bible gives us *parthenos*, a text echoed in the Matthean infancy narratives, the Hebrew original from which it is taken has none of the implications of *virginity* with which the later texts are associated'. The class were bent under over-bright institutional lighting, leafing through different versions of Isaiah, comparing and contrasting, Lucy doing battle with her highlighter. One bright spark, a relaxed looking blond American chap, piped up 'and so, the entire doctrinal edifice of the Virgin Birth has been erected on a faulty premise?' Angela was gratified 'Indeed... the whole tradition stands or falls on the translation of that single word.' David was taking notes by hand, looking slightly concerned. 'The dualistic Platonic influence is clear' she went on, 'although, of course, that does not oblige *us* to be dualists! The writers of the Hebrew texts would have had no problem with sex.'

'*Gosh,* isn't this radical stuff?' David was pushing closer to Lucy now, moving towards the coffee machine, breathing a little too heavily for her liking. She was flushed and excited, more so than she'd been for a very long time. 'She's quite a performer, too, isn't she?' He was still hopeful of a response. Wanted to carry her with him in his enthusiasm. And someone said, within earshot, 'yes, isn't she magnificent?' Lucy could feel the eagerness all around her, was not sure whether she was simply conforming, but heard herself agreeing, rather too quickly for her self-respect. 'I've learned more tonight than I have in years,' her tone was unaffected; 'I think I'm beginning to understand... how complex these things are.' Lucy had crossed a threshold. And her monthly Retreat at the Abbey, scheduled for next weekend, would give her time to think it over. She needed to talk to Sr Agatha. She hadn't known such stimulation for years.

'So you see, St Teresa divides up her treatise on prayer into seven sections,' Sr Agatha was in full flow, getting down to business. 'The experience of prayer is like a journey, it goes in stages… progresses. Or perhaps a better analogy would be *a relationship*. Teresa, however uses the image of a castle (in Freudian terms a very feminine symbol, although Teresa would not have known that) a mansion composed of seven 'dwelling places', at the heart and centre of which God Himself dwells alone. Our task is to get to the centre.' Lucy put her copy of The Interior Castle to one side, wondering how she'd ever got herself into this kind of maze. There was something almost Kabbalistic about the imagery. And would a cloistered lifetime really allow her favoured access to the inner chambers of the castle, perhaps it might impede it? 'Only pure love can penetrate to the centre of the castle', Agatha concluded. 'That *pure love* is offered us, by the grace of God.' And the bell rang for Sext.

The next few weeks were a busy time at the Orlando Press; Bloomsbury was lurching from one deadline to another and there were interviews and readings still to do. Lucy's agenda of tasks yet undone was becoming frighteningly long, and she would not be able to make it to the lectures for a couple of weeks. Overtime at the office was not even an option; it was a necessity. And she may even have to miss out on daily Mass; the Lord would understand. She'd catch David at church on Sunday and ask him to save her some handouts. She could catch up on the reading later.

And so another year had hurtled towards Christmas. There had been the usual procession of mince-pie heavy festive gatherings, office fancy dress, and carol-singing in the parish events. Wine tasting of cloves. Lucy had even had her hair cut, to express the more experimental turn her life was taking… the enrolment on the course, the intellectually questioning (*heuristic,* as Angela called it) approach, the successful establishment of appropriate boundaries with David. And all against the back-drop of a longer-term project with the Abbey; the sisters had given her two more years to finish her course and make a decision. She'd be thirty-five by that time, old enough to know her own mind, and with her MA under her belt. They were all agreed on that.

It was one of the earlier January days, the streets heaving with post-Christmas shoppers, their hands heavy with brightly coloured sale bags and unwanted gifts. Angela Fowler had wandered almost aimlessly into Waterstone's, the massive, fortress-like establishment on Piccadilly. The busiest part of the season was past and she found she had a couple of hours to kill before Evensong. She'd invited Dr Coverdale to preach, a courtesy gesture more than anything else, but it let her off the hook for one more day, and was the reason for her relative relaxation of mind as she browsed the self-help manuals and the New Age magazines, her thoughts fixed on nothing in particular. It was then she remembered she'd promised a copy of Vita Sackville-West's study of the two Teresas, *The Eagle and The Dove*, as a coming of age present for one of her nieces; the family still had these oddly pagan practices. And Melinda was precocious. She'd have a coffee and make her way to the theology section... no hurry; these places were open half the night.

It was as she was passing the travel section that she heard the familiar voice, not loud but quietly insistent and measured in its tones. The gaps between the words strangely equal, creating the impression of tranquillity. And a familiar fragrance; was it Rosewater? But Angela saw nobody she recognised, just a small family engaged in some minor dispute at the side of the cash desk, and a couple of anonymous young adults, their backs turned. Lucy, meanwhile, had been investigating Avila, examining its castles, surveying its ramparts, all with a view to a trip there in the spring. Do it while you can, she thought... get out a bit and live. She'd written David off now; happiness did not lie in that direction. But first she'd go and have that coffee.

The two women had been standing next to one another in the queue for some minutes, before Angela's phone went off and she'd muttered in that husky, rather rapid tone of hers, rummaging hectically through the contents of an over-large shoulder bag. Smooth green leather. Damn it, she'd missed it. Must reset the ring-time to a longer stretch to allow for situations of mental abstraction. Or the inconvenience of public places. Or turn the bloody thing off. It was as she was negotiating this difficult process that the younger woman spoke to her and she started, irritated at first, and then, the look on her face changing to pleasured recognition saying 'Oh Lucy! I didn't see you standing there! Or rather the hair! Wow, I *like* it. What's with the change of image?' Lucy ran two brave fingers through the graduated bob, a gleaming bowl of chocolate-brown above the still serious face, a face now lighting up, animated and flushing with the frisson she felt at the prospect of this unexpected change of plan, an afternoon with Angela? Or at least a coffee and a chat. *My God*, she'd missed her (Lucy suddenly realised) and the input of the weekly lectures.

'Okay, so let's have the whole story,' the cropped woman was saying, rather too loudly for the younger one's comfort. They'd opted for Smoothies, not coffee, and were at the window seat, leafing through travel brochures and phrase books, intimately engaged. David decided to let it pass; he'd move on to another table, did not want to intrude (again). It was then that he noticed the signals that had escaped him at first; Lucy, clearly engaged in confidences, was speaking rapidly and more intensely than usual, the older woman's hand cupped over hers in a gesture of solidarity on the hard Formica surface. He took his copy of The Republic from a rather shabby satchel, together with a couple of Kleenex, and turned his chair away; he'd be better off facing the wall. When, forty minutes later, he rose to leave, having retained nothing of his reading, he turned again and saw their fingers linked, their faces now serious, quietly intent on one another. He was leaving the refreshment area when Lucy arrived at the counter to order the Cappuccinos. But he'd gone, and was out of earshot by the time she called after the barista to say 'and make them both no sugar!'

'So, Lucy, you've decided to make the trip with a friend?' Sr Agatha was groping for details. 'Yes,' Lucy said, her eyes wide under the heavy, smooth brown hair. There was definitely something different about her this time, Agatha thought, a new kind of grace and energy. And Lucy had shown her the brochures, the turrets and towers of the Castilian plain. The visit had gone well. Lucy had not told them everything; just that her sense of direction was changing. She'd done the Eucharistic Retreat again this year, had found it moving but blander than before. Just an enfolding kind of peace. Nothing she could describe as consummation.

Now, she sat with her newfound friend, their fingers interlinked, on the Thirty Bus. They were nearly at Stoke Newington and the rustle for the exit had begun. But the two remained seated, waiting for the hubbub to subside. The younger woman was rummaging for keys, and, the bus finally empty, passed them, a plain set of three on a neutral-looking key-ring, to her friend with a wink. 'If you could go ahead and open up, I'll pop round to Vitelli's to get us a bottle of red. You could start heating up the ciabatta.' And they smiled at one another.

Angela had got the hummus just right, lots of garlic and

lemon, and warded off a couple of phone calls. She was in the process of lighting some candles when the spare key turned in the lock and Lucy appeared, triumphant with three bottles, not one. 'Special Offer!' she exclaimed, pulling off an over-heavy winter coat. 'Phew, it's cold out there.' Angela, already stripy-aproned, pulled her towards her, with an affectionate laugh, 'and *you* need warming up.' Lucy, suddenly relaxed, dropped her gloves, one by one, to the floor, and divested herself of her magenta scarf, commenting how nice it was to come back to candles. And to olives. 'There are plenty more where those came from' the older woman said. 'But first... you must come here and tell me about your prayer life.'

Noel Williams

The promise of proof

The only time Gethyn and I hitched together,
down from Bicester to Bath,
we pitched the tent off the A420 before Swindon.

And the stars. The stars poured into the sky
like foam on the tides of darkness, as if I lay
dazed by the skirts of angels.
I was young then, perhaps fifteen.
Skirts were often in my mind. But not this,
this lace of light in a carousel, a whirlpool.
I was lifted from that damp verge
and swung into the dance.

Another day, above Coniston, Carrol and I
came onto a tarn startled with dragonflies.
I'd never seen one.
Here, hundreds scooped and slipped,
splinters of the silver of our first summer.
I waded in scribbles of light, fragments of skating glass.

I don't offer these as proof,
but they may have been promises.
In any case, I'm someone else now.
But they had the shape of music, orchestration,
delights somehow planned within an astonishing maths.
Dragonflies as stars.

Declining silence

The world, I guess, grows heavier.
Your look makes light of it,
refracting through pools still as prophetic stones
creased by quick fishes of hope.
So how can I do this to you?

I remember you in a stranger's garden
open to the moon,
naked under a filigree of alder
or a rowan, perhaps. That won't happen again;
no matter how often I rewind it.
Laughter and silence meant the same
though neither could be translated.

Did I mean what that silence said?
It may be the time to discover
whether my silence lied, or whether
I am the man I could be,
made by, with and for you.

David Ford

Man with rain on his back

A white shirt,
sudden storm.
This is what
that summer was like:
promises,
exclamation marks,
the spluttering
of Gods rage
across our shoulders,
tears, small
cotton tears.

Grand mal

We step away from my sister, push
the furniture back, give her space.
She is acting out a mock death,
eyes rolled blind like a roman bust,
body shaking with uncontrolled passion,
back testing whether it can break,
my father's finger in her mouth.

This is our dirty secret.
We wait for her to come back to us
from the intense, secret place
that pins her to the floor with its beauty.

fff

A child is running towards the camera,
always the photographer is pulling away.

*

Your face in close up on a crumpled sheet—
dark face of a saint, a smudge, an aura.

*

His father throws him up into the air,
he rewinds it again and again
his father catches him with open arms.

*

The movie of our life—
the film sticks in the gate,
burns from the outside in.

*

Film shows on winter nights, the curtains closed,
a makeshift screen. Happiness replayed in ektachrome.

David Batten

As I Age

I notice I begin to disengage
withdraw deeper into the holt of me

on an autumn night hunters' rifle fire
seems very close now their season started

the visitors gone the guns broken out
lovingly rubbed cleaned and clicked and click clicked

wolf-haunted hounds on the starvation scent
stealthily take up my train of thought while

bullets pass through part of me on the way
to the remaining bewildered wildlife

year 0

i know that deer
stepping into the shadow

the trickling
of this brook

the smell
of these plants and these

the snoutings of pigs
from the undergrowth

that disappearing
snakes tail

this trapped
and bloodied hare

that eagle
with which i cant compete or compare

ive made it my business
i even seem to know these cattle

but not that far off insect
coming nearer with the crash of falling trees

what is this long gentle thunder and white line
fraying over me sky unstitching

The Clockmaker's Daughter
Jennifer Bailey

My father gave me the stones, oval shapes smoothed by the stream near the house he'd grown up in. He gave me the bird's nest that was collapsing to dust, the small blue-grey eggshells, the catapult he'd carved, three polished pennies and a tiny china figure he'd found while digging for potatoes in his own father's vegetable garden.

My father's hands were broad with square nails and calloused skin. Together we stacked the stones into asymmetrical towers or we arranged them in patterns under the white lilac tree. If I stroked them along my cheek, they generated warmth.

While my father was dying I arranged the stones, the china figure, the nest holding blue-grey eggshells, the catapult and pennies along a shelf in the garage. I memorised their position before hauling the garage door closed. At night, always at night while he was sleeping, I took the torch and examined these treasures. I bent close and checked for movement, for a concealed magical life. It was something to believe in. It passed the time.

Mr Stirzaker was a friend of my father's who came to our house every Sunday for his dinner and ignored me; not that I minded. I'd watch the men eat what I'd cooked, noticing my father's comforting clatter against Mr Stirzaker's delicate silence. After, I'd take them tea on a tray then leave them to it. So if my father hadn't told me I'd never have known about Mr Stirzaker's daughter, Ruth.

'He doesn't say much about her.' I remember I was tucking the rug round his legs when he said this; being that close to him made me think of Ruth as a character he'd invented to fill the moment.

'Why?' I asked. 'Is she a secret?'

I smiled to show that we were sharing a joke, but my father's gaze swivelled.

'He's not very pleased with her. He says he can't think of her as being a real part of his life.'

'Why?'

My father raised his shoulders, and his expression was closed and tight.

We didn't talk about Ruth again.

After my father's death I was surprised when Mr Stirzaker said it was no good me being on my own and why didn't I come to live in his house. He'd told my father about his great-grandfather who built the house and how it was surrounded by farmland and woods; how streams seamed their way into the soft earth. Then streets of brick terraces were built, corner shops and churches; and eventually, the mosque.

The offer didn't appeal, though I could see there was kindness in it, made out of the feelings he'd had for his friend. But he was thinking of the rent as well. My father had talked about Mr Stirzaker being short of money, because he had a shop in town which took clocks and watches for mending and there wasn't much call for that any more.

'He's a clever man. He doesn't just mend watches; he makes them and beautiful things they are. Not cheap either.'

That impressed me; it made sense of Mr Stirzaker's delicate hands, the intentness of his eyes. And eventually I did go to live in his house because he was right, it wasn't any good me being on my own. On the very first day, when I was carrying a box up into the attic rooms he'd let me have and thinking that I might turn right round and leave, there was Ruth leaning against an open window. She told me who she was, then pointed downstairs and bugged her eyes. Our joined laughter sounded like friendship, so I didn't stop her from looking at what I'd already unpacked. She picked up one of my father's stones arranged on the mantelpiece and pushed it against her lips which muffled her voice.

'I don't live here. But my father gave me a key so I come and go, though I'm not allowed to bring anyone over.' Then after a bit she said, 'I mean; we don't talk much.'

We talk though, Ruth and me, or rather she talks, just about every day. The way it goes is that she's here by about mid-afternoon when she's finished her shift as a hotel receptionist and before Mr Stirzaker is back from the shop. She talks about everything, for instance, when her parents split up. She talks about the house a lot and I pick up that really she's talking about her father who she loves just about better than anyone and who she wants to be with, especially because he refuses her. By now, I know why he refuses her so that if she wanted, she could do something about that, but I don't say so.

In fact, I don't say much. I never have. Instead, I watch; that's what my father called me, a watcher. Today I'm watching her try on my clothes. She puts something on then pulls it off after a glance in the mirror, taking her time to fold and add it to one of the tidy piles on the table.

Because it's Mr Stirzaker's birthday, he's having some people round for tea and cake. Ruth has bought him a woollen hat, which I've wrapped in tissue paper, and a card which we've both signed.

She bends close to the mirror and brushes on mascara. 'My father believes in birthdays. He says the older you get, the more you need to keep track of things. He says marking time slows it down.'

I think that time drags enough as it is. Early on a midsummer morning my father died while I was arranging pink tuberoses in the cut glass vase he'd picked up in the market. There was sunlight on the back lawn, the grass was a lemony green and I decided it was warm enough to open the kitchen window.

Then she swings round like she's remembered something. 'I never asked whether you've got a bloke.'

I shake my head, keeping the movement brisk. Ruth pulls me to the mirror and we stand side by side, I'm in a black skirt and sweater, her in bra and pants. I stare at us both, how shadowy I look against her bright white skin.

'Listen, you're pretty. Mahdi has friends who're really OK so d'you want me to check?'

'No. No thanks.'

'Is it because he's Muslim?'

She's sharp and more than ready to be offended so I say, 'Of course not.'

Though it is, but not for the reasons she'd expect. I don't think I can find the words to explain why Mahdi's world is not one I could be part of.

Because of Mahdi Gurmani, Mr Stirzaker will go days, even weeks without speaking to Ruth, but he speaks to me. Brewing a pot of tea, slicing bread, he talks about his dislike of Asians. He calls Ruth a fool and spittle flecks his bottom lip; when he flings a knife into the sink, the noise makes my heart race. My silence aggravates him because he wants an argument.

'Don't stare at me like that. Your own father didn't think any different; he told me many a time he'd not want you to mix with people like that.'

Part of me wants to see this as proof of my father's protectiveness, wanting to keep me safe from the world, while another part knows that's wrong. So I'm caught in a dilemma. I can't go back to the way I remembered us together or go forward to who I could be now.

Ruth pulls on her coat, opens the window and leans out. I join her. She lights up. There's been a rainstorm, but now dark clouds give up the sun into a clear stretch of sky. I watch how everything shines wet up here; roof-tiles, gutters, drain-pipes. I watch water drops falling to where the puddles are flashing like mirrors. A man passes on a bike that wobbles as he balances a loaded basket on the crossbar. I pull my watching up to the sky again, which makes me think about when the sun will disappear, not temporarily behind a cloud but for good. One second blue sky, bright light, warmth and then nothing. That's it. That's how time passes.

Ruth turns to me.

'I'm going over to Mahdi's.'

'You'll be late for the birthday tea.'

'Not by much. Come with me.'

I shake my head then check her reaction. But when I look at her wide-open eyes, all I can see is how moist they are and how they reflect the sunlight. She flicks her stub into space. Then she ruffles through a pile of clothes and picks out a blouse she's already rejected, one I last wore years ago. It has a peter pan collar with short puff sleeves and the pale pink cotton is patterned with flowers. She wears it with her jeans.

We go downstairs and passing the kitchen doorway, Mr Stirzaker glances at us, but doesn't pause in his birthday preparations. He has a pet yellow bird he calls Sarah, which sits on his shoulder, wings half-spread for balance. When he smiles at it, I think that the only unconditional love some people can feel is for animals. And birds.

We come down steps into the street and Ruth turns left towards Mahdi's house; I go the other way, taking the streets at random. A man on a chair in his open doorway holds up his arm in a salute. I walk fast as gets darker.

The rain begins just as I get back to the house. People cluster in the hall, leaning close as if telling secrets. Others wander between the kitchen and front room, where Mr Stirzaker has covered his dining table with a yellow checked cloth. Surrounded by plates of party food, the birthday cake he's made is iced and wrapped around by a frilled band decorated with snowmen and

Santas. Cups and saucers are stacked on the sideboard.

All of Mr Stirzaker's guests are old men and they ignore me. I imagine they're his loyal customers who've kept him in business. No-one is eating or drinking so I know I'm more or less on time.

I go upstairs to collect Mr Stirzaker's present and card then sit by the front room window to watch the street. Mr Stirzaker comes in, sees me and smiles in welcome, as if I'm a surprise guest. I smile back. My jaw aches, but I can't unclench it. A movement on the front steps catches my attention and there's Ruth with Mahdi following. Mr Stirzaker leaves the front room.

'Bugger off!' he shouts.

I follow everyone into the hall.

He's holding the front door open and they're standing just outside, both of them with wet slick hair because it's raining hard now. Mahdi's skin is so dark that when he lifts his head to stare at Mr Stirzaker, the whites of his eyes are luminous. Mr Stirzaker steps forward, but Mahdi doesn't move. There's a long pause when nothing happens, just the yellow bird singing from the kitchen.

Then Ruth says, 'Daddy,' like she's telling him something. When she goes towards him, he walks upstairs and she follows. Mahdi stares ahead, but it's hard to know what he's thinking until he turns his back and leaves. Someone shuts the door. The present and card feel sticky because my hands are so hot.

When they come back down stairs Mr Stirzaker has his arm round Ruth's waist, as tight as a belt. Wearing jeans and my blouse with the Peter Pan collar and puff sleeves, with a smile spilling from the fingers pushed in her mouth, she looks a girl. She looks like me. I hold out his present and card, and push between them.

Nicola Warwick

Fetch

Sometimes I think I am a ghost,
not really there, I haven't been seen,
a chill in the air.

When you pass me in the street,
we exchange a breath
and you shudder, as if
a cold hand had travelled
down your spine.

Sometimes, I am the wind
that keens in your ear,
a skitter of leaves,
the whisper of a bee in passing.

But I never was there. I am see-through,
a not-quite-there, the rattle of glass
in a window, a door that doesn't fit,
a will-o'-the wisp.

Incubii

They told us, the old women,
that if we went out at night
we'd meet them, those men,
in dark places where love is unmade.

They told us that these men
would be beast-like
and rowdy, we'd know
what they were by their smell.

They told us, if we willed it,
if we neglected our duties
we'd be visited by nightmares
that would weigh on our chests.

They told us we'd vanish
for a while, a few hours,
before they'd let us come back
to our homes and we'd be changed.

They told us the first time
would be a spoiling, a damage,
we'd be tainted with blood
and fierce bruises.

And they told us we'd suffer
being reckless if we went
with these men and any offspring
we had would be faulted.

So they warned us, the old women,
we'd be impure to the bone,
unwanted and fouled, the prints
of their hands would always mark us.

St Etheldreda

After sixteen years, they dug up
the coffin I'd chosen to reflect
my faith, thinking it long enough
for time and worms to do their work.
They expected little more than bones
to wash and bless for interment
in the church.

They recalled my last days;
falling in and out of fever
as the tumour gnawed my neck.
As a child, I'd cherished the touch
of beads on skin, the cold shock
of gold or a light amber kiss
at my nape.

They remembered my end,
the surgeon lancing the growth,
the ooze of blood wreathing my neck
with gore. The fever seemed to pass,
returned on the third day as I slipped
into peace.

So, they'd expected little to be left.
But here was wonder.
They lifted the lid, then stopped,
felled to their knees at the sight
of an uncorrupted body,
the gape in my neck
closed to a soft mouth.

Mariana Rueda Santana

Quebrada Seca

They ran to the highest point of Quebrada Seca,
The fifty nine of them
running from the river, the sea; anything.
They huddled together for one day,
mostly quiet, wondering why the apocalypse
decided to come a month early.
(At the strike of the millennium
would have been made more sense).

The first helicopters came at dawn to take photos.
One more day and more helicopters came.
When rescuers stepped on the land it sank like flan.

On the Hill

He did not leave
even when the firemen came to gather the last few families.
He watched the mountain sides
melt and run
stripping the land of trees,
re- dressing all in a commotion of limbs,
bricks and diarrhoea.

He watched the corpses being pulled out
twisted at odd angles, dripping bistre.
He pictures their lungs of mudsoaked sponge.

The church held up,
so did the statues of the saints
who emerged with glassy eyes
looking up to heaven

Lyn White

Porziuncola Retreat House Bahar ic Caghar, Malta, July 2008

1

It is the coldest corner in the place.
I plan another visit, a slip down
after dark to lie on the floor
realign my spine against marble tile
tease the spaces between vertebra
back to position, throw out hot arms
splay scorched legs, doss down
right there, in the aisle
blatant, in front of the altar
femaleness, flagrant in gratitude.

2

Heat has raged away
as if all this island manages
is a small circumference
unable to spin out of the dazzle
of a stationary sun. Even its night
bears gold from day as metal,
tried in fire, scalds long after
withdrawal. The ink from the pen
seems to hiss then evaporate
faster than I can put words on a page.

Jogging philosophy

Taking a walk with Demosthenes today
I enquired about stammers and stones.
He told me philosophy and oratory
were not ideal careers for a stutterer.
The bulk of what exists in the head
must be said for maximum impact.
So, just sometimes, his reflection
clear in the water makes him think
he would have preferred
beachcombing instead of a life
hammering out wrinkles
in his vocal chords, reciting poetry
with a mouth full of pebbles
running breathlessly, yelling
above the sound of the sea.

Phil Madden

White

Kurdistan: it is a busy day for the mother of the bride. She must inspect for red. Her mother is losing her mind and her sheets must be cleaned. There are still some guests, snoring.

Cyprus: It is the first day of the honeymoon. She has changed from white into crimson. The walls reflect the sun. The widows are gossiping shadows.

India. There is wailing. He was much loved. Wrapped in white he will be burnt to the sky like clouds.

Cornwall. The sheet cracks and billows in the spring frost air. There is a yacht far out to sea. The sheet whips to be free.

The Morgue. The body is peaceful and blanched.

The Torture Cell. Please may I have a cup of tea before you begin. From the finest porcelain. So I may compose myself into white song.

After the words were said. I will paint the walls white. I will sell the ornaments. We will never speak of this again.

In My Heart. There is the white book you gave me. Your first gift. I will never write in it.

Land Mermaid

Today the clocks go back.
It has been raining.
The beach is deserted.
 Waves woo.
This would be a good time.
I put pebbles on my clothes.
Strike out.
Far out.
Last look.
A woman is walking her dogs.
She throws sticks on the sand. They chase them.
She throws sticks in the water. They will not enter.
She sees me. Waves.
A land mermaid.
Calling. Calling.

Sightlines
Helen Holmes

You didn't hold it against me that I killed your wife. On the day I came into the world and she left it, you became almost as devoted to me as you had to her. For some fathers, the nappy-changing, bottle-sanitizing, carrot-mashing routine would have paved the way to disenchantment; for you, it cemented our relationship. You swiftly sainted my mother. 'An English rose,' you sighed, caressing photographs warped and smeared by years of adulation. 'She was,' you said, hoisting your shoulders in that eloquent Gallic shrug, 'too good for this world, Thérèse.' You never remarried; I stayed at home. It seemed the least I could do.

When you roared to your death on the A38 on your ancient Norton, you left me Adolphe the bi-lingual parrot, fifty-seven bottled ships, a pile of bills and an ache as deep as the Atlantic.

When Adolphe and I were learning to speak you differentiated your material in line with best pedagogical practice. With me, you sashayed between decorous English and '*comme il faut*' French as the whim took you. With Adolphe, you resurrected the jubilant obscenity of your sea-years. And you taught him to bark. Insurance-averse, you judged this a useful security measure. A knock at the door might be greeted by a barking dog, a foul-mouthed Frenchman or an abusive Englishman with a faint French accent. Adolphe captures to perfection your Gauloise-gravelled voice. It's comforting to hear you swearing at me.

The house is much as you left it. You were never interested in keeping up with the latest fad. Our décor was minimal before there was a name for it. I've colonised your sagging armchair. The bright rugs you haggled over in far-flung bazaars are fading to pastel, the wooden floors mellowing to a richer gold. The shells round the mantelpiece mirror are slackening like snails losing traction. Your bedroom is home to rainy-day washing and sedimentary layers of teaching silt.

I've been sitting at the workbench in the back bedroom staring out at a blurred wilderness. When you set up our workshop, the garden was a sight for sore eyes: pillows of French lavender; glowing geraniums; the vegetable patch with its bamboo wigwams and pots of mint and creeping thyme. I must have been about four when you picked up maple salvaged from a wreck in Plymouth. You spent days sawing, planning and sanding. When the bench was in place, I crept into the resinous room and scrambled up. I stroked the silky wood, feeling for blemishes with my fingertips and sneezing out tickly dust.

Together, we fashioned our flotilla. You assembled your regiment of instruments, long-shafted tools with wooden handles. 'Forceps, please,' you would say, 'Tongs.' 'Large probe.' Your fingers were like spatulas, but you worked with delicacy and precision. You sculpted putty, peering through half-moon glasses teetering on the end of your nose. You conjured up wave-tossed water with Prussian blue and turquoise acrylics. You layered the deck, cutting, gluing and impatiently leaving to dry before stroking on burnt umber and lamp black. My favourite part was mast-building which, in time, you delegated. I attached the fragile spindles, collapsing them umbrella-like along the deck of the hull. As the ship slipped clear of the neck of the bottle, I eased the sails and masts upright, tugging gently on threads of cotton, scarcely daring to breathe.

'Hi, Thérèse. This seat free?'

'Oh, hi there, Cath. Yes, it is. Good summer?'

'Brilliant, thanks. Son and heir's wedding, followed by a fortnight in Spain recovering. Now we're recovering from all the Rioja. You?'

'Oh, I just mooched about here.'

'Uh-oh. Here comes our revered Leader. What thrills and spills does he have in store for us this term, I wonder.'

'I wish they'd focus that projector,' I say.

'I can see the words,' Cath says. 'Making sense of them's more of a challenge. What the hell does 'capitalising on downsizing' mean?'

'It's all a blur to me.'

'Where ignorance is bliss, dear.'

Nothing saps the spirit like a mizzly Monday morning. I know how the kids feel. In they shuffle, shoulders hunched under outsized rucksacks, heads down, eyes averted. Some are honing excuses for uncompleted homework: pet sabotage, family bereavement, a litany of biblical misfortunes. Others are processing the weekend's legacy: the hot date, the new haircut, the row with Mum, Dad's violent homecoming. If we make it to lunchtime, surviving the week will begin to seem feasible.

'*Bonjour, la classe.*'

'*Bon-jour-Mad-mwa-zel-Dor-on.*'

'*Vous avez passé un bon weekend?* Robert?'

'Wha'? Er... *Oui.*'

'*Qu'est-ce que tu as fait?*'

'Er... *j'ai allé...*'

'*Je suis allé.*'

'*Je suis allé...* er...'

'*Au cinéma? Au match de football?*'

'Er... *oui.*'

'*Bravo*, Robert.'

I take refuge in the staffroom. Cath hands me a steaming mug.

'You look knackered. Crap morning?'

'Not great. Is Robert Sinclair in your tutor-group?'

Cath pulls a face. 'Too right he is. I must've been dreadfully wicked in a previous incarnation.'

'It's not just me, then?'

'Idle, arrogant, spoilt little toe-rag. Thinks he's God's gift.'

'He's going to come a cropper in French next year if he doesn't get his act together.'

Cath chortles. 'What planet are you on, Thérèse? Why should the very wonderful Robert Sinclair be arsed to learn French when everyone who counts speaks English? That'll be his take on it, trust me. Thinks we've still got a bleeding empire.'

You first took me to the optician's in my last year at primary school, when I couldn't see the blackboard from the back of the class or the numbers on buses until they loomed over me. Speccy four-eyes. Digging out my most recent prescription from the dusty depths of the bureau last night, I was staggered to find it was eight years old. No wonder I'm blind as a bat.

*

'Can you read the bottom line for me?'

'I'd be guessing.'

'No problem. What about the next one up?'

'Z-O-E-C-F-L-D-P-B-T.'

'Well done! Now I'm going to plunge us into darkness. Which dot can you see more clearly, red or green?'

'Red.'

'Super! And now?'

'Green.'

'Great!'

Enthusiastic Emily passes me over to solicitous Simon, who will help me choose new frames.

'Let me look at your face,' he commands, staring unnervingly.

'Heart-shaped,' he pronounces, 'delicate bone structure, straight nose. Try these for me.'

'No,' he says, 'they dominate your face. Try these.'

'No,' he says, 'the bridge needs to be a touch higher and narrower. Try these.'

'The shape's good,' he says, 'but we need a subtler shade with that creamy skin. Try these … Oh, yes! Look.'

The pale, angular face is all too familiar, but the frames are transformative. Simon is good at his job.

'Your astigmatism makes your prescription more complex,' he explains. 'I would recommend thin lenses, with an anti-scratch, non-reflective coating, to show those big green eyes to full advantage.'

The price is eye-watering.

I must tuck up the garden for winter. But on the other side of the unruly hedge lurk creaking Mr Bates and his limping Labrador Moriarty, with needs masquerading as offers of tea and exercise.

'Come on, then, old chap,' I say, clipping on the lead. 'Walkies. We'll go through the precinct, Mr Bates, and I'll pick up your tobacco and milk. The Gazette's out today—I'll get you one, shall I? If we turn down into the park and go round the duck-pond, that'll probably be enough won't it?'

'Plenty, I should think. He's very stiff, so take it gently. I want whole milk, mind, Thérèse. None of that gnat's piss.'

'I know. Come on, then, Moriarty.'

Moriarty has died. Mr Bates is heartbroken. I invite him in for coffee and watch helpless as fat tears worm through the furrows on his face. My platitudes comfort him as little as the meagre offerings doled out when you died. I hold his hand at the kitchen table and stroke his skin with my thumb, feel bird-bones under blotched transparent parchment. Tomorrow, we'll scatter

Moriarty's ashes under the sycamore where he used to shelter on hot days.

When you accelerated into oblivion, I dug a cupful of your gritty dust into the soil under a lavender bush. The rest I cradled in a lurid plastic urn to our favourite spot by the sea. I rolled up my trousers and waded into the shallows, submerged the container. But you refused to leave. On the third dunking the apologetic waves washed you away. I sat in the dunes gazing out to sea until the cheery dog-walkers began to arrive with their genial halloos.

Mr Bates sighs, drags a white sail out of his pocket and mops his face, trumpets his nose.

'Drink your coffee while it's hot,' I say.

He sips. 'That's the real McCoy, isn't it? Takes me right back to holidays in France with Muriel. Lovely.'

Mr Bates accompanies me to the Garden Centre and trundles my trolley past spotted wellingtons, Christmas decorations and bird-feeders like miniature Swiss chalets. Just starboard of a coach-load of pensioners devouring cream teas, we home in on baskets of onion-like bulbs, skins papery to the touch. We dither over narcissi with sunny hearts, purple crocuses, tulips like frilly cream knickers. I screw up my eyes to read the labels. The small print quivers queasily. I must decide on new glasses. I could ignore Simon's advice and opt for a cheaper package: thick, scratchable, reflective lenses in bargain basement frames, which will show my big green eyes to least advantage. But something in me rebels. Mr Bates drops our selection of bulbs into brown paper bags and twists the corners tight.

The garden is beaten into submission. Mr Bates helps and hinders. As night closes in, I heave pots into positions where I'll see them from the kitchen, living-room, and bedroom. I print names neatly on lollipop sticks and ease them into the soil. Come Spring, I'll be on the qui vive for pale green shoots piercing the black loam.

My Head of Department wants to see me. I wonder what I've done wrong. He normally leaves me to it. It's not Appraisal time. I go into his classroom at break.

'Ah, Thérèse, thanks for popping in. I won't keep you. I just wanted a quick word about Robert Sinclair.'

I groan.

'I know—a right royal pain in the *derrière*. His mum's very concerned about his progress in French.'

'She's not the only one, Geoff. He's a bright lad, but completely unmotivated.'

'Thing is, Ma Sinclair seems keen to get to grips with young Robert. She's been on the phone to ask if I can recommend a private tutor.'

'Oh.'

'And I wondered…'

My instinct is to say that I'd rather have nails driven into my eyes than spend a second longer with Robert Sinclair than I contractually must. But then I think of those glasses.

'Well…'

'You don't need to decide now,' Geoff says. 'If you're willing to consider it, Mrs Sinclair suggests discussing terms over coffee on neutral territory. No commitment on either side.'

'I suppose that can't do any harm.'

'She strikes me as a sensible woman.'

Headlights stream towards me, swerving away inches from the café's glass wall. The wet pavement, acid yellow under the streetlights, flashes neon red and blue. Inside, it's warm, the lighting subtle, the walls unpainted plywood panels. My woollen skirt slides on the smooth surface of the aluminium chair, making me push myself upright. I squint again at my watch. Ten minutes late. I'll give her another ten. The clatter of the coffee-grinder competes with mood music. The first stage of your daily ritual was to grind beans in that antique contraption you picked up in some French flea-market. I'd watch as you added water to the base of the heavy percolator, spooned powder into the receptacle, screwed the two halves tight and set it on the gas. Minutes later it would belch and gargle and fill the kitchen with the aroma I'm inhaling now. I'd got lazy about coffee. You'd have been horrified.

The door swings open.

'Miss Doron? Hi, I'm Celia, Robert's mum. So sorry I'm late. The phone rang just as I was leaving the office.'

She looks a little older than me, fortyish, elegantly draped in muted greens, grey eyes framed by matt black metal. She removes her glasses to wipe away sudden condensation and gazes at me myopically.

'Many thanks for agreeing to meet. Let me get you a drink. Then we can talk about that embarrassing son of mine. Coffee?'

Posh, you would have said, pronouncing it 'poash', half-ironically. Scones were 'scoanes', too. You liked to take the mickey out of the English bourgeoisie. But Celia's terms are generous.

I'm transfixed by my reflection in the crumbling mantelpiece mirror. The quality of customer care at the optician's has been impressive. Having stared, tweaked, stared, adjusted, stared some more, Simon has finally declared himself satisfied, but has insisted on one more appointment in ten days' time. To make certain that the fit is perfect. Once the glasses have settled. Settled? I only remember one fitting last time, but that's so long ago that my memory may be playing tricks. And Simon is a perfectionist. His eyes are the colour of forget-me-nots.

I can see Adolphe glaring at me. His inky pupils are dilated, the whites Daz-advert blue.

'What do you think of my new glasses, then, Adolphe?'

'Fuck off.'

'Oh, come on. Lighten up, you miserable old buzzard.'

His response is a maniacal cackle. 'Anchors away!' he shrieks. 'Full steam ahead!'

Kaddy Benyon

Call it Love

She asks you what it could mean
that you want to touch the deep

orange curves of her mind; that you
find yourself begging, bartering,

performing for a portion of her heart.
She says you may never know

what it is to be loved, if you can't tell
first why you smile when she trips

on words unready for speech; why
her frown makes you hurt for the soft

rock of her hips; why you are shaken
by forgetting her teeth, her lips,

the shelter in her voice. You do not
know why you are afraid of the dark,

dark red of her clogs; of the bark
inside her coughs; why you want

to howl when she greets you first
on Thursdays in low sleepy vowels;

why you want to curl up inside her;
why you want to curl up, inside her.

Fitzwilliam Selkie

after *Wave Spinning* 2008, by Maggie Hambling

Find a museum, a bookshop, a park
when feeling mournful, all at sea.
Sit on a bench, hold tight, invite
nobody in with words or eyes or sighs,
just be—be still in the flotsam
of crashing moods, believe in the selkie
(her silk kelp skirts and impish smile),
let her slowly surface from behind
oil-spattered spindrifts, loop
your pale fingers through the curve
of her elbow, rest your head
on her shoulder while she sails you back
to life, surfing a blue-green vein
along the estuary of your wrist.

Oliver Comins

Sweet Seventeen
Short poems for a flexible, modern family home

trees, an old building,
nothing is moving out here,
even this river

*

where our children play
their arms reaching in and out
blown leaves shimmering

*

cold days piling up
with tasks we never started
working late again

*

from one foreign land
to another, no road sleeps
beneath these wheels

Firethorn (*Pyracantha coccinea*)

So little light left, seeping into the rooms
Where we live with long nurtured needs,
Our favourite toys and journals scattered
On rugs and floors we should have tidied.

Red berry, yellow berry: each bush seems
To be growing more confident as the days
Draw in, the nights stretch, their deepening
Colour an antidote to winter's draining.

Residents and itinerants gather to feast
On a choice of wholesome pomes around
Sharp barbs—yellow berry reaching over
Into number thirty five's reluctant garden,
Red berry soaring a few yards to the west,
Alternative sunshine for number thirty one.

Nigel Pickard

Being a Man

You walk behind the bearer who carries
the box your baby boys are both to be
buried in, and I'm staggered that you manage
it. One foot then the other. Moving, like
that. At the edge of the grave, you clutch your
wife to stop her being swallowed too, while
small children from the next-door school spill out
happily to play. I find myself

having to look away. At the fields that
light and wind scour like time's speeded up. At
the rest of those present, who equally look
this way or that. And yet afterwards in
the pub you are there again, still upright,
still holding your wife. Saying you know where
the boys are. That's the thing, if it doesn't
sound dense. No. You're still—somehow—making sense.

House

What I like about this house is the clear
simplicity with which it has been put
together. There's no pretence: the limestone
walls, the red-tiled roof. It is as you might

draw a house when a child, three square windows
on the first floor, three oblong ones on the
ground, a white door and a beard of ivy
in between. Once inside, the whitewashed walls,

the hulking beams that hold it all in place. You
can see the age of the wood, its heaviness,
the way it fits as if nothing else could.
We walk across cool stone floors and look out

over sunflowers and fields of corn, watch
birds stitch the patterns of trees and the grass
shift with crickets. Then in the distance, there's
language—we hear it, but it is not ours.

Bonanza Tully's Baby
Joanna Campbell

Bonanza Tully left her baby by the river the day of the pig roasting. It wasn't a good place. Slimy silver gravel. All those sinking holes. I could see the pram, a creaking crate on wagon wheels, was lopsided already. She'd only just walked away from it, striding up the bank in that way she had. One arm crooked, fingers splayed, hips rocking like a pendulum.

I waited for her to turn round. I was hot through, like the sun was spearing my back. But she kept on walking. She was as far as the double oak when I knew she weren't coming back any time soon.

Seems like I spent my entire life waiting to see her, then closing up like a startled clam. But today was different. Decided that at sun-up.

Didn't know if she'd seen me at the shack there. I'd fancied her eyes were on me for a fraction. But I was sort of tucked in the rotting porch. I was pondering my new direction, the broken wood splintering my backside. And she'd appeared. My heart did a square dance up against my ribs. Same as always, but with a new twist. Like a floozy in red net skirts wriggling her shoulder at you and winking.

I'd heard a squeak in a regular kinda rhythm. I'd thought mouse. Clamped in the jaws of a feral cat. I wanted to take it in the shack and make a nest with that bit of stiff blanket stuck to the damp boards.

But it was pram wheels. I think Old Man Tully had kinda nailed them on all anyhow. Whisper is that he pilfered two from Josh Napper's buggy and the others from Zuleika's Hardware. Those wheels hollered as they turned like piglets on a stick. With each turn the square-dancing floozy cranked up her pace.

The pram had been stuck there a fair time when the early sun broke through the timbers. I felt Clem Coffee's tread flattening the grassy bank behind me. The cattle slowly raised their heads, glistening with dew, curling down their eye-lids against the glare.

'You been with Bonanza?' Clem's breath was hot on my face as he swung in a great arc on the porch strut. I wished it would give way.

I stayed silent.

'She got that swine basted yet, d'ya think?'

'I guess so, Clem. She's done it every July since she turned ten years old.'

'Looking swell, ain't she?' Clem was eating his Ma's cake, jaws threshing away like a combine.

We all got this photograph at school. Marking the end. A city man like a mole in a sweating collar came with a tall hooded camera. Her face is near worn away on my copy. Bonanza was right by me that day. Hair like silver rain. I threaded through the huddle to get to her. Miss Mather, lumpy face all screwed up, said it was right enough having the dumbest in the same row. I rubbed my thumb over Bonanza's grainy face at nights. Got me to sleep. Ready for a new start. Once my courage was up and skipping.

Clem kicked at a pile of ants, exploding them into streaks of ragged black goin' every which way, hard at it.

'What's that doing there?' He flicked his head at the pram and spat out the caraway seeds stored in his mouth.

I stared at the frayed blouse Clem was wearing. It was his big sister's. His Ma turned her girls' stuff into shirts for her one boy. It still had a frill on the edge of the collar. He'd tried to fold it under. And it was pink.

I willed the strange wheezing from the pram to stop.

I could do that. Make things happen. Didn't always work. Didn't stop Old Emmanuel Tully trying to fish naked for dabs from the roof of his barn in the moonlight.

The noise stopped. I unfocused from the blouse. Clem let out a few more seeds. He pulled off his clothes and strode into the river. The ducks fussed and started the pram whining again. Clem forced his stocky brown body into the depths and disappeared in the green film.

I inched my behind a little ways off the porch. Babies round here get ignored mostly, left to grizzle, but this one was in danger of listing into the river. Ten minutes would do it. That could mean I got to see Bonanza again real soon. She would have thrown it right in if she'd wanted it drowned.

Folk here said it had two heads on account of being sired by her daddy. Couldn't believe that. Emmanuel was soaked in scotch night and day. Ever since he stopped burrowing out that new tunnel. Saw the minerals in a vision, he'd said, beard frothing with spittle. Had a stake in a good mine, but sold it quick, squandered the cash. Then he was after discovering his own little pocket. Like thousands of others camped out in their potato-sack tents, whisky bottle chimneys poking out the top.

'Richer veins,' he would roar, strutting through the seamed land as though he could see clean through the earth to the silver below. 'Feel 'em vibratin' in my soul.' And off he went scratching the mountain dirt for colour. Buried ore ain't easy to find.

He became superstitious. If a magpie swaggered across his path, he'd grab a gun.

He cursed the sticky blue soil on his pick. Didn't recognise silver ore worth two thousand dollars a ton. A blind man searching, he was. His baby daughter became the only bonanza he would know. And he used her up same ways as he wasted his cash.

Clem surged up and shook like a cur, a thousand rainbow drops flying from his hair. He loomed out onto the mud, paraded a bit, cocky, watching for Bonanza to come back. I fixed my eyes on his skin all raised up in pimples. I willed her to come and give him the hard eye. Wither him.

'Could be mine,' he crowed, thrusting his thumb at the pram. 'Haven't seen the thing yet. Sinkin', ain't it?'

The pram was quiet. Higher up through the trees came a striking and a rustling. We turned.

Bonanza was sparking up her fire in the clearing, sat facing our way astride a tin pail with her pale skirts and petticoats all bunched out around her and her long slender feet planted on the earth, toes curled in. Her arms were like ribbons, but they worked like a miner's, on and on, sparking that fire, stopping only to set up her spit.

Through the trees the sun shafted onto her as she worked. We heard the echoes a second after she made the movements. Her milk-laden bosoms faltered above her bodice as she rubbed the sticks together. I thought Clem, shining and naked beside me, would burst. The pair of us, taut and silent, watched the fire blaze into life.

I saw her look up, skin flushed, a patch of dirt on one cheekbone. Clem slunk behind me and coaxed his trousers over his damp, shaking legs.

I looked at Bonanza and I saw answers. I was gonna take her with me. I was willing it. I'd get myself a job in Virginny City. Maybe in a newspaper office. Smallest ant on the hill. But I wouldn't trek back home at nights. I'd find us a boarding house.

106

Some were dirt cheap. I could sit at a counter while Bonanza nursed the baby. Leave my beer behind and be a man.

She looked at me again and her lilac eyes were soft like ma's stewed plums. Huge and liquid. They were saying something. Was she telling me to get rid of Clem? He was in a fix with the crotch of his trews, cursing and jumping like a summer bull-frog.

'Clem!'

We both froze. It was his Ma.

I snuck a look up to the track, glimpsed her red plaid shirt, meaty arms crossed over it. He was in for it. Always was. I twisted to look at him, saw his fretted brow.

'Done your chores, Clem?' I asked him.

'What the hell do you think?'

'Clem!' She was louder now. Set the cows lowing and pacing. 'Clem!'

Then there was an echo. Except it wasn't.

'Clem!'

Bonanza was calling from behind her flames. Her face was distorted by the smoke. I fancied she was smiling in a kinda beckoning way at Clem. But it was the bleary way the air goes when there's a fire. Made her face pucker. Made me feel dizzy. Weak.

But she was callin' Clem right enough. And his Ma was hollerin' louder. Then Bonanza was standing and shouting and smiling. I felt Clem break into a sweat.

Bonanza was playing with him like a kitten with a shrew. He looked shrunken. His teeth were clattering. His Ma called again. There was a slopping sound as the pram slid deeper into the mire.

Clem ran. He rasped past my shoulder and to his Ma. I heard her cuff him round the head.

Loser. Blouse Boy.

Bonanza was throwing back her head laughin' and she called him again, making him look round. And he did, even while his Ma was tuggin' on his blouse sleeve and fair draggin' him homewards to his chores. Bonanza had her back to me then, but I swear she tore her chemise open, mocking him some more. No surprise. Her body had been portioned out so many times 'gainst her will. Far as I knew, it didn't have anything to do with her no more.

I only knew the girl inside the skin. I knew the Bonanza who nursed old folk and cooked for them that couldn't raise a potato. Spoon-fed them too, she did. Young and old. All the dribblers and

107

moaners. She helped with birthing babies. If there were screams in the black of night, Bonanza would run from the bed in the corner of her kitchen.

When she birthed her own kid, she laboured alone, folk said. No one lifted their ass for her.

Bonanza stoked up her fire again and grinned at me. Her hooks and eyes weren't fastened right yet. I knew she wouldn't tease me like she did Clem, but there was something different today.

I looked hard when she leaned away to pick up her jar of basting grease. She had a battered leather bag there. I could see it through the smoke. It had a yellow ribbon tied in a bow on the handle. Baby stuff, I guessed.

There was buzzin'. Folk coming for their roast. Bringing beer and vegetables, calling to Bonanza about the pig.

'Can't smell nothing, Bonanza! Where's that baby hog?' Zuleika was shrill, jowls wobbling like underset jelly. 'Remembered the mustard?'

'If that pig's still sucking on its ma I'll skin you and spear you on the spit instead, my girl. Got enough on you to baste yourself, ain't you, eh, ain't you girl?' Emmanuel was staggering down the bank with his night cap still on and his bottle broken, jagged at the neck. He wiped the blood from his beard.

Josh Napper had a gang, the Fist Boys, with him. They were jostling for a good place to sit and drink. Josh's Pa was tied in with an ore pocket that was making a mint. Josh had a cooked chicken, a scarlet silk cravat and a basket of whisky. He pushed past Emmanuel and yelled at Bonanza to spike the hog. He didn't look at her though. No one did.

They were lookin' at the pram.

The sun was blasting through the shack now. Sweat was weeping down my back and springing out on my forehead. Smoke was scalding my throat. I swear I could breathe in Bonanza too. I knew her smell. Her smell was toil and suffering and pain and pride. I could take her away now. Let her smell of apricot roses all day and all night.

But I couldn't move. I watched as she stood to grapple with the roasting spit and anchor it over the flames, testing out the ground, checking it was solid. It wasn't. Too boggy here. No base for a heavy piglet to turn on. Wouldn't be the first time she'd lit a second fire in a better place. Keep the first for baking squash. She had her hands on her hips. This was the time.

I stood up, hanging on to a post, a bit rickety from last night's ale.

That was when the wagon wheel croaked into the mud and the damn pram tipped toward the water. Sun blazed on the black paint. There was no sound. I took a step. Bonanza didn't move.

'I'm havin' my wheels back!' Josh was showing off, gathering his cronies.

'Bonanza Tully, get that stinking crate out the mire and hand over my wheels too!' Zuleika's flesh was leaking out of her black frock. She leant on the shack and I felt it quaver.

The town was pouring down like an ant colony on the move. Searching for their hunk of pork, drooling, smacking their lips, waiting for full bellies.

Except Emmanuel Tully.

He didn't know cock-crow from moonshine. He knew his girl needed bullying, is all. That and his hopeless quest.

'Richer veins I'm getting' me today, boys. Better than your Pa's piss-hole pocket, Josh Napper. Thicker seams. Gettin' myself outa here.' He was roaring above the fire, above the creaking, above the sigh of the great wind goading the flames.

It was a rash wind, ours. Quickened up the clouds from the west, blocked the light and rocked the pram right over. Turned upside down in the river and starting off downstream.

Zuleika screamed like a spanked toddler and the Fist Boys looked around. I sank down kinda heavy. They all stared at me. Josh was shock-fixed on the bloody bundle emerging from the pram and floating fast away.

'The pig,' he said in disbelief. 'Been breathin' its last in there. Throat weren't slit all the ways through.'

I took another step. Bonanza was looking my way. The shouting started. Lads jumped in to get the wheels, directed by Zuleika and Josh.

The rain came, nailing us to the spot, Bonanza and I. She picked up the bag with the yellow bow and eased it a bit more open. She held it up to show me a little baby in a white suit, waving its fists at me. She kicked at the drenched fire and it left a dirty plume of smoke between us.

When it cleared, she was already stridin' up the bank in her way, wet dress clinging to her legs, the bag cradled in one arm, the other cocked as usual.

I knew there would be a bus on the main street and I knew sure as hell she'd be catching it. It was her dream to get the hell out of here. Just like it was mine. Only she was doin' it.

'That girl ain't got my coffee ready. I can't walk straight without my coffee. Got myself a long ways to go before daybreak. Git her back, boy. Got my plans and she knows it. Git her back here now! Wait up gal. Wait up!'

Her Pa was grunting out the words, almost pitiful, it was.

But Bonanza was walking. On a mission for her own self. Long paces up to the town with her little baby. Thin sliver of sun peeking back out again between the clouds, right on her hair.

Folks were picking up the pig. Thinkin' of their bellies. Rollin' their stolen wheels back home through the soaking grass. Fighting over the spit and the fire and the drinks. Fists were flailing around.

I thought of Bonanza's white skin and silver hair that I had never touched and her baby with a face like a lily. She wasn't coming home again, I knew that.

'I'll be shovellin' out dollars.' Emmanuel was grabbing arms, telling folk about his new silver seam.

They all knew there'd be no bonanza. Another borrusca. Bust.

But Old Man Tully cackled into his beard, placing his palm over the neck of his bottle to keep out the rain. He saw me for the first time.

'Drink, boy?'

I couldn't move my backside from the shelter of the shack no more. My leg hurt like hell. Needed beer to dull the pain. Lost the other in a cave-in down Yellow Jacket Mine. Just came clean off. I can stand on one leg, but that don't get you far. Cave-ins killed a man a week, so I guess I was lucky.

Today wasn't different no more. Old Man Tully corked up the bottle and tossed it over. The cattle raised their heads as I caught it and then lowered their eyes to the grass.

Marcus Smith

Before Words

Before words your hands told the story,
pointed the way right to your heart,
a path running straight as desire,

and pure sound splashed everywhere,
stomping in puddles, racing through
forests of tall gutturals shaking

dead leaves from our shrivelled sky.
Other language—your dark-eyed
reaching for things we had forgotten

or couldn't translate—made all words
pale copy on greying paper.
While you laughed colours and cried

deeper than red, blue and black,
how we longed to shout real oaths
to the sun, unlock those voices

jailed in our muted souls, afraid
they died, leaving merely words.

Why We Go

...The pigeons are window-shopping
and stores are closed on Sundays so moms and dads
will stay home and play parents with their kids.
Why is that man with holes always lying
on the sidewalk? It's dirty. Isn't he cold?
...Yes, but why doesn't he have a pillow?

Look! Bus 47. I love to go
seeing the sea lions after we hold
Baby Jesus in church. Alleluia!
Alleluia! Jesus is a nice carpenter —
he makes crosses and loves fish and beggars.

Look. A tree stump — it used to be a
tree. Maybe it was the Burning Bush.
I like to hear stories. Is that why we go?

Bill Trüb

Anonymous

In 1981, he fell out of his mother
and pattered feverish zigzags
into the carpet. In '83, he formed
neon nouns in his mouth. By 1990,
he'd invented invisibility

and no one saw him for a decade.
In 2001, big-bellied and love drunk,
he stepped into the world in a wig,
almond eyes behind sunglasses.
He wanted to be a she

most Mondays. In the fury of 2003,
he met his match and promptly
destroyed it. He wanted to be the first
to tell you this but he tumbled off-track
and grew comfortable in the thorns.

In '04, he ran against Jesus
for president of the world
and lost. Barely. So he stole steel
and built a time capsule, filled it
with unfinished business—an archive

of a man's abortions, a tribute
to a prince of very little.
He buried it in 2008 and now
waits for someone to dig it up
and, finally, give him a name.

Painkiller

That bloodshot lady, throat coated
in quicksilver, her son, that queen
with quaaludes, yeah I know them.

You could say I made them rich
before I wrote headlines
for their tombstones

and licked the marble to numb
my gums. Look at me: perfect
damage. My brain goes rat-a-tat-tat,

zip-zap. I can sell you this feeling.
You got my number, I'm that brown-eyed
failure with no fingerprints and a killer

smile, always here to help. Just ask.
I can write your headline, too,
and it will change your life.

Embers

He lacked three things: self-identity, survival skills, and a killer instinct.

I led him to Diamondback River, where rapids unfurl over stone. He stood on the bank, peered into the water and saw his face for the first time. A rippled blur of Adonis.

He grew hungry. I showed him how to feed a fine line through a hole, knot it, then shank the thin hook into a night crawler. There'd be a pop of blood, I warned. I showed him how to lift the rod skyward and cast the line. He marvelled at the arch. 'Adjust the slack. Wait 'til you get a bite.'

The red-and-white bobber soon sunk and, with an upward jerk of the rod, the hook pierced the lip of a rainbow trout. We pulled in our catch, watched it breakdance on sand. We scaled it, filleted it and had dinner—as did the fish, its belly full of earthworm.

At midnight, I introduced him to the moon—its face was deadpan, pockmarked, trustworthy. The man was unimpressed. I told him I'd teach him how to build a fire if he could find kindling. He unzipped his jeans and mine and rubbed together the branches.

Sparks birthed a small blaze. He knelt, blew on it, grew it. He stepped back, let the flames take me, then slept by my warmth through the night.

In the morning, he revisited the river to see how big he could smile.

Contributors

Josh Ekroy's poems have appeared in Envoi, Smith's Knoll, Rialto, Other Poetry, The SHOp and others. Some war poems will feature in Stand 2011. He won first prize in the Bedford Competition 2009, third prize in the Keats-Shelley 2009, was commended in the Poetry London Competition 2009 and Ver Poets 2010.

Jennifer Bailey was born and brought up in Lancashire and now lives in London where she teaches theatre to American undergraduates. Her publications include a book on Norman Mailer, a number of reviews, and critical articles. Her short stories have appeared in Writing Women, Slow Dancer, Sheffield Thursday, and Staple.

David Batten has taught poetry and creative writing at Coleg Meirion Dwyfor, won the inaugural *Roundyhouse* poetry competition and has now been twice short-listed (last 10) for the Cinnamon Press Poetry Collection Award. His fifteen minutes of poetic fame include being asked by Carol Ann Duffy to read one of his poems at her reading in Machynlleth, and helping to put Matthew Sweeney to bed at Llanystumdwy, for which he received a peck on the cheek from Jo Shapcott: he now lives in France.

Kaddy Benyon worked as a television scriptwriter prior to having children. She started writing poetry in 2009 and her poems have appeared in Spilt Milk, Mslexia, London Magazine, Popshot and are forthcoming in The Frogmore Papers and Stand. She was shortlisted for both the 2010 Fish Poetry Prize and the inaugural Picador Poetry Prize.

Sharon Black is originally from Glasgow but now lives in the remote Cévennes mountains of southern France. In 2010 she won the The New Writer prize for Best Poetry Collection; in 2009 she won the Envoi International Poetry Prize and The New Writer prize for Best Single Poem. She has been published in various magazines including Mslexia, Envoi and Orbis.

Jacci Bulamn was published in South Bank Poetry magazine, Forward Press anthology, short-listed for Bridport prize, second in Mirehouse poetry competition, published in 2011 Cinnamon Press anthology. Inspired by people, she tries hard to keep her poetry clear and within reach. She is currently learning from Stevie Smith and Leonard Cohen.

Joanna Campbell writes short stories all day at home in the Cotswolds, with three cats and occasional bowls of cereal for company. She has been published in various magazines and anthologies. In 2010, she was shortlisted for the Fish, Bristol and Bridport Short Story Prizes.

Catherine Coldstream was born in London and educated in the West Country and at Oxford. She has studied viola, composition, and theology, worked in music publishing, and spent twelve years as a nun in an enclosed contemplative community. She now lives in Oxford, where she writes, performs, and teaches.

Oliver Comins lives and works in West London. Poems widely published in magazines and also in Feeling the Pressure (British Council), 'Playing out Time in an Awkward Light' (a pamphlet from The Mandeville Press) and Anvil New Poets Two.

David Ford was born in Devon and lives in East London. His work has been widely published in magazines and a pamphlet collection was published by the HappenStance Press in 2010

Kate Fox has performed her work everywhere from Aldeburgh Poetry Festival to BBC 2's Daily Politics Show and is a regular on Radio 4's Saturday Live. She won New Writing North's Andrew Waterhouse Award in 2006 and is still working towards a full collection which might mix comic and less comic poetry and has been drip dropping out onto the radio, stage, publications like Magma, Under The Radar, Aesthetica and her pamphlets from Ek Zuban, Zebra Publishing and New Writing North. She's a 35 year old Northern reformed radio journalist, this year's Poet in Residence for the Great North Run and interacts erratically online via www.katefox.co.uk

Helen Holmes started writing for pleasure after a career in Education. A recent MA in Creative Writing at Newcastle University revved up her idling brain. She has won a New Writing North short story competition and was shortlisted for a Mslexia competition. She lives with her husband in North Northumberland.

Janet Holst is a New Zealander currently living in Oman. She has taught in Melanesia, New Zealand, South Africa and the Middle East. Her stories have been published in South Africa and Australia, and academic articles in various journals.

Amy Kellam

Phil Madden lives in Wales. He travels   Europe as a Disability Consultant .His work has appeared in many anthologies and magazines. He has written two limited edition books   "Wings Take Us" and" 39 Faces of the Urban Moon" with   renowned engravers Paul Kershaw and Peter Lazarov.

Jane McLaughlin writes poetry and short stories. *A Roof of Red Tiles* is the title story of this anthology. Her work has appeared in several other Cinnamon Press publications and in a wide range of magazines and anthologies. She wrote a series of poems about the Titanic disaster after visiting Halifax, Nova Scotia in 2010; two of them are published here.

Sue Moules has appeared in several Cinnamon anthologies. Her most recent collections are *In The Green Seascape* (Lapwing) 2009, and *The Earth Singing* (Lapwing) 2010.

Nigel Pickard is the author of a poetry chapbook, *Making Sense* (Shoestring, 2004), and two novels, *One* (Bookcase, 2005) and *Attention Deficit* (Weathervane, 2010).

Mariana Rueda Santana is a Venezuelan-born poet based in the UK. She has a Master's Degree in Creative & Critical Writing from the University of Gloucestershire and works as a copywriter. Her poetry has appeared in *The Sandhopper Lover & Other Stories & Poems, Envoi, Desire and Madness and Under Surveillance.*

Rosemary Shepperd is studying for a PhD at Glamorgan. Her poems have appeared in magazines on both sides of the Atlantic and she was one of five finalists for the Manchester Poetry Prize.

Marcus Smith's work has appeared in *Ambit, Acumen, PN Review, Prairie Schooner, Salzburg Poetry Review* and *The South Carolina Review*.

Inventor of words, amateur platypus spotter and Sabina's daddy, **Bill Trüb** teaches literacy in South Africa. In other lives, he has chased students for homework in New Jersey and dug up earthworms in Wales. He holds an MA in Peacefully Rocking Your Face Off. His friends, who wrote this biog for him, call him Liam and Weirdo.

Louise Warren is a poet and playwright. Her poems have been published in Agenda, Envoi, Fuselit, The Interpreters House, Orbis (featured Poet), Obsessed by Pipework, Poetry Monthly, Stand, Seam, Poetry Wales and The New Writer. She was in the Ver Poetry Prize Anthology 2008. Her poems have also appeared in a number of anthologies. Louise is the winner of the 2011 Cinnamon Press first collection prize and her book *A Child's Last Picture Book Of The Zoo*, which will be coming out in 2012.

Nicola Warwick lives in Suffolk where she works in local government. She has had poems in various magazines, as well as prizes in competitions. She has twice been a finalist in the Cinnamon Press Poetry Collection Award.

Lyn White is the librarian of the guest library at The Friars, Aylesford, a 13th century Carmelite Priory in Kent. Her poetry has been published in a variety of journals and anthologies. She is heavily involved in establishing a writer's group with the Hazlitt Theatre, Maidstone.

Noel Williams is widely published in anthologies and magazines, including *Iota, Envoi, The North* and *Wasafiri*, and has won fifty prizes and commendations. He was Resident Poet at Sheffield's Bank Street Arts Centre, with a highly successful *exhibition, Exploding Poetry. He's a lecturer and a student at Sheffield Hallam University, and runs writing workshops for local organisations. Website:* http://noelwilliams.wordpress.com/

Martin Willitts Jr poems appear in *Storm at Galesburg and other stories* (international anthology). His tenth chapbook is *The Garden of French Horns* (Pudding House Publications, 2008) and his second full length book of poetry is *The Hummingbird* (March Street Press, 2009. He is co-editor of www.hotmetalpress.nert

Patricia Wooldridge lives in Hampshire and is inspired by landscape and nature. She has a doctorate in creative writing and until recently taught creative writing to undergraduate students. Her poetry has been published in a variety of poetry magazines including *The London Magazine, Interpreter's House, Iota, and Staple.*

Megan Wynne-Jones is of Welsh heritage. She grew up in England and now lives in Australia, in the Blue Mountains. She has been writing for as long as she can remember and her poetry and fiction have been published in Australia.